SURVIVING THE TOXIC WORKPLACE

PROTECT YOURSELF Against the Co-workers, Bosses, and Work Environments That Poison Your Day

LINNDA DURRÉ, Ph.D.

New York Chicago San Francisco Lisbon London Madrid Mexico City
Milan New Delhi San Juan Seoul Singapore Sydney Toronto

The McGraw-Hill Companies

Copyright © 2010 by Linnda Durré. All rights reserved. Printed in the United States of America. Except as permitted under the United States Copyright Act of 1976, no part of this publication may be reproduced or distributed in any form or by any means, or stored in a database or retrieval system, without the prior written permission of the publisher.

1 2 3 4 5 6 7 8 9 10 11 12 13 14 15 16 17 DOC/DOC 1 9 8 7 6 5 4 3 2 1 0

ISBN 978-0-07-166467-7
MHID 0-07-166467-X

McGraw-Hill books are available at special quantity discounts to use as premiums and sales promotions or for use in corporate training programs. To contact a representative, please e-mail us at bulksales@mcgraw-hill.com.

Staff Infections is a trademark registered by Linnda Durré.

This book provides a variety of ideas and suggestions for dealing with people in the workplace; it is not intended to serve as a replacement for professional advice. The information in the book is the author's own opinion, unless otherwise stated.

Contents

PART I

STAFF INFECTIONS

What They Are and How They Hurt You, Others, and Your Company

CHAPTER 1

Why *Surviving the Toxic Workplace* Can Help You, the Economy, and the World

Do you dread getting out of bed each day and dealing with bosses and co-workers who drive you crazy? Are you surrounded by people who are incompetent, negative, verbally abusive, and impossible to deal with? Have you asked the human resources department for help, yet nothing changes? These are all signs of Staff Infections—the difficulties you experience in dealing with toxic people and workplace conditions. Welcome to the reality that millions of people face on a daily basis. If it feels as if you are living in a "Dilbert" cartoon some days, then you need this book! In it you will find important information that will empower you to change your work environment, psychological explanations of the toxic behavior you experience, and, most important, techniques to remedy situations with obnoxious and difficult co-workers and bosses. After reading *Surviving the Toxic Workplace* and understanding how to communicate and be assertive, hopefully you'll be able to enjoy your job, get along with people, and have a productive, rewarding, and satisfying work experience in a safe and protected environment.

This book is important to companies as well as individuals. On a larger scale, it could benefit the world economy. Companies lose billions of dollars each year because of miscommunication, poor time management, alcoholism and drug addiction, high turnover, and lowered productivity. The reverberations from any single incident could be catastrophic, resulting in costly lawsuits and court-imposed fines. This book will show you how to change such situations, stop them, and prevent them from happening again—no matter if you're an entry-level employee or an executive.

Whether we're in a flourishing, abundant economy or a recession, good communication skills, assertiveness, and cooperation are essential to running a company. In a recession, these traits become even more crucial because many times there are harsh cutbacks, with employees doing the job of two or even three people, hours and benefits are slashed, and tension, stress, and problems arise.

I will address these issues by first describing effective communication techniques and instructing you how to communicate with co-workers yourself. If my suggestions don't work, then it may be necessary to report the difficult co-worker to the boss or HR. Granted, there are times when it is mandatory to seek assistance from a supervisor and the head of HR. Try my techniques first before going to a higher level. Nobody benefits from being perceived as a helpless whiner, so it's up to you to solve these challenges—using my proven techniques.

In some instances it might be necessary to confront your boss about his or her own difficult behavior. Obviously in this depressed economy you don't want to get fired. However, a confrontation won't necessarily translate into your losing your job. Find an example in this book that reflects your situation, and use it to your advantage. Be as tactful and diplomatic as possible while remaining clear, firm, and assertive. Practice the words beforehand—perhaps in front of a mirror—until you feel comfortable. You may even want to tape-record or videotape yourself, then review the tape to find your weak spots. You may also want to ask close friends, your partner, spouse, or a colleague for feedback. Remember, you have a right to a happy, hassle-free workplace—one that is free of distraction and discrimination.

Many people feel helpless and hopeless in confronting problems at work. They are thwarted at each turn by a rigid administration that doesn't want change, stifles open and honest communication, and makes trouble for people who make any attempt to speak up. In some companies, HR may side with the management against the workers, so your complaints could be squelched even further. It's true that this can be frustrating and painful, and in a bad economy, most people don't want to rock the boat. So you have a choice—keep quiet and put up with it, or say something to remedy it.

If you keep quiet, you will increase the stress you feel, and you might even begin to hate going to work even more. Such a tense emotional state can bring on physical ailments such as migraine headaches, backaches, ulcers, and high blood pressure. On the other hand, you can learn to speak up, be assertive, and confront the situation directly in a variety of ways. If direct communication fails to effect change, you can also explore other options to solve the situation—reporting it to HR, alerting the union or professional/trade association, publicizing it with the media, seeking legal help, and filing a lawsuit or a class-action suit. Websites and contact information are provided in Chapter 38 and on my website for reporting violations to federal agencies. I hope all of the information in the following chapters helps you to remedy a negative situation so you can work in a cooperative, productive environment where you enjoy going to work!

CHAPTER 2

Are You in a Toxic Company Dealing with Toxic Co-Workers?

If you feel you are working in a toxic work environment with toxic people, take this quiz to find out:

Are you doing the work of two or three people and paid one salary? . . . . YES NO

Do you resent working harder and longer than your co-workers? . . . . YES NO

Do you get little or no appreciation and thanks? . . . . YES NO

Does a co-worker drive you crazy? . . . . YES NO

Are you/another in danger at work because of unsafe conditions? . . . . YES NO

Have you/another asked your boss or HR for help or made a formal report but nothing changed? . . . . YES NO

Are there dangerous conditions at work that go unrepaired? . . . . YES NO

Does a co-worker have disgusting personal habits? . . . . . . YES NO

Does a co-worker often interrupt your work? . . . . YES NO

Is a co-worker chronically late yet no one says anything? . . . YES NO

Does a co-worker miss deadlines and affect productivity? . . YES NO

Does a co-worker steal your ideas and take credit? . . . . . . YES NO

Does a co-worker ask you to cover or lie for him or her?. . . . YES NO

Does a co-worker act like your boss when you are peers?. . . YES NO

Is a co-worker criticizing your work constantly for no reason? YES NO

Does a co-worker go on political rants and no one stops him or her?. . . . . YES NO

Does a co-worker get on a morality/religious soap box at work? . . . . YES NO

Is someone at work having an affair and you have to lie for him or her?. . . . . YES NO

Has a co-worker set you up to take the blame for his or her mistake? . . . . YES NO

Have you ever been asked to falsify data, reports, or documents?. . . . . YES NO

Have you ever been asked to do anything unethical, illegal, or immoral? . . . . YES NO

If it's a family business, do family members get away with things that others don't? . . . . YES NO

Have you/another ever been sexually harassed at work? . . . YES NO

Does a co-worker use sexual favors to get ahead at work? . . YES NO

Does a co-worker tell lewd jokes in front of you and others? YES NO

Are people surfing porn websites instead of working? . . . . YES NO

Have you ever heard someone tell a racist joke at work? . . . YES NO

Have you/another ever been discriminated against because of race, ethnic group, gender, age, religion, or sexual orientation? . . . . YES NO

Do people come to work drunk or high and no one says anything? . . . . YES NO

Is a co-worker late or missing deadlines because of alcohol or drugs? . . . . YES NO

Has a co-worker ever threatened you or assaulted you? . . . . YES NO

Has there ever been workplace violence? . . . . YES NO

If you answered yes to just one of these questions, you may be working in a toxic company with toxic co-workers, a toxic boss, or an ineffective HR department. This book will help you identify the toxic behavior, understand why it happens, and empower you to confront it. Learning the components of communication, assertiveness, and active listening will assist you in being diplomatic, clear, and firm when setting limits and establishing boundaries with your toxic co-workers and boss. It will show you how to approach a co-worker by starting off positively, delivering feedback, asking for specific behavioral changes, and ending positively. This book will give you a feeling of power and affirm your right to deal directly with an obnoxious co-worker who is interrupting your productivity, disturbing the work environment, and possibly endangering you and others. You will learn the necessary tools to approach your boss and the HR department to ask for changes, report a co-worker, or file a complaint.

And if that fails, other options are available to you—including, but not limited to, filing a lawsuit, filing a class-action suit, going to the media, and using your union, trade or professional association, the state licensing board, or government agencies such as EEOC and OSHA to advance and settle your case. This book can identify workplace problems, give you the knowledge and power to change them, and help all workers and companies eliminate toxic behavior to work cooperatively, productively, and safely. Making positive changes will increase productivity, raise morale, and spur profits.

I wish you and your company the best to succeed in a positive, happy workplace and marketplace.

CHAPTER 3

Staff Infections

The Negative Effects They Have on a Company

If you're reading this book and you've taken the quiz in Chapter 2, then you're probably working in a toxic environment with toxic co-workers—just like millions of other people are doing every day around the world. Do you dream of a new job where the goals are clearly defined, your co-workers and supervisors are honest and cooperative, and you are appreciated for your contribution? You can find such a job or create it for yourself. You can start your own business by yourself or with people you know and trust, or you can even work alone. But before you jump into the self-employment fray, read on and find out how you can transform your present workplace into a better one.

You may be the only one who can stop the toxicity from continuing, so you must develop the courage to stand up to the bullies, bigots, and bozos at work who intimidate, annoy, and stymie you. The toxic circumstances may have been going on for so long that you are used to them and, like an abused child, you have learned dysfunctional ways to cope. That needs to stop. In an office setting, just as in a dysfunctional family, each person learns to deal with the craziness when the entire office actually needs an overhaul. Also similar to that difficult family, one individual in an office setting can see the dysfunction, change his or her own approach to dealing with the family of toxic employees, and make that overhaul a reality, changing the dynamics into a more positive, healthy environment.

Aside from taking the quiz, there is a lot more to learn about identifying the toxic conditions and signs of what I refer to as Staff Infections, my program to remedy toxic companies, so that you can know if you're experiencing them. Once we've identified the situations, we will discuss methods to change them.

What Are Symptoms of a Toxic Work Environment?

Negative effects from toxic behavior can include many of the following situations. See how many you can identify in your workplace and in other businesses where you've been employed:

- Managers avoid dealing with and correcting problems brought to them by their employees. Problems only increase and get worse when ignored.
- The office suffers from unusually high absenteeism, which occurs when people call in sick too often to avoid coming to work. They get ill, need a mental health day, or play sick when they may actually be looking for a new job because they're so unhappy.
- Employees seem as though they want to quit and instead set up bosses to fire them, so they can collect unemployment and maintain their insurance under COBRA.
- There is a high rate of transfers to other departments, divisions, or branches occurs because of a toxic boss, department head, or co-workers.
- Gossipmongers set out to destroy someone's reputation through rumor and innuendo and sometimes succeed. Gossip causes fear, dissent, resentment, paranoia, and rebellion.
- Inhibitive and petty company policies restricting lunch hours, communication, socializing, dress codes, and so forth, create an angry, resentful workforce.

- Cheap and incomplete health insurance, which can be a cause of great employee resentment, happens when a company promises more than it delivers and workers are angry to discover that certain insurance claims are not covered when they thought or were told they were.
- People are prevented from being hired or being promoted seemingly because of their gender, age, sexual preference, race, religion, or ethnic background. Discrimination provokes toxic resentment in many ways.
- Sexual harassment creates a hostile work environment, causing work interference, resentment, avoidance, and possibly lawsuits.
- Personality conflicts impede progress on projects and productivity altogether, which leads to lower profits, canceled contracts, and high turnover.
- Strange habits of co-workers that are distracting, disgusting, or illegal keep the work from being completed, deadlines from being met, and the environment from being peaceful, thus costing the company time and money.
- The problems of alcoholics and drug addicts are ignored. They are not sent to rehabilitation or residential treatment with a 12-step program.
- Alcoholics and drug addicts cause injuries, accidents, and even deaths, resulting in the company paying millions in insurance claims. Lawsuits arise because people have been victims of alcoholics' and addicts' toxic and dangerous behavior.
- Building code violations and dangerous work environments are reported yet nothing is done about it—the building is not up to safety code, paint is peeling, elevators don't work properly, and more, which can cause accidents and even fatalities. Lawsuits arise because toxic conditions are not remedied quickly and completely.
- Workers feel danger because certain employees are on the edge and have demonstrated signs of mental illness, as well as suicidal or homicidal tendencies, yet nothing is done to get them help.
- Security in the building is lax. It seems as though anyone—including disgruntled former employees–could slip right in, undetected, or falsify security badges.

- The evacuation program and prevention drills are not up-to-date, so if a disaster were to hit, lives, equipment, and data could be lost.
- Product liability lawsuits, stemming from a careless mistake such as toys with traces of lead, cost companies millions of dollars and endanger consumers.
- Teamwork and morale are low or nonexistent, and dissension is everywhere.
- Deadlines, production quotas, and final goals are not met, thus losing credibility, reputation, and business.
- Mergers with other companies or departments may have unclear restructuring plans to consolidate positions and possibly terminate employees. Without a clear plan, exact job descriptions, and delegation of responsibilities, this type of reorganization will inevitably inspire resentment and dissent.

All of these are symptoms of Staff Infections—dysfunctional behavior in the workplace. Sound familiar? Ignoring these problems doesn't make them go away. Denial, minimization, and procrastination are common but ineffective and ultimately dangerous coping mechanisms to deal with these challenges. Each of these toxic behaviors, all of which are explored and examined in Part III, can be remedied when handled quickly, tactfully, and effectively. If confronting the problem yourself does not solve the situation, then it's time to discuss it with HR. Finally, if HR doesn't handle it, then you have to seek outside options: filing a complaint with the EEOC, OSHA, your union, trade association, or licensing board; going to the press; or getting an attorney, filing a lawsuit, and taking your case to court. In most instances, though, it should never come to that, and it doesn't have to.

Why and How People Cope with Toxic Companies and Co-Workers

Many businesses and corporations operate with chronic problems and it's a wonder how they keep going at all. Employees put up with hostile and negative environments because they have bills to pay and children to support. Fear of losing one's job is the number one reason problems at work persist year after year until every day is like an episode of *The Office*—without the laughs. Welcome to Crazy Town. Managers and directors ignore problems, thinking they will go away or resolve themselves. Many owners and high-level managers do not have the time to deal with problems and assign others to do it, and the delegation of duty fails. When the VIPs finally do get around to looking at the problem, it may be too late.

The cycle repeats over and over—toxic behavior, passing the buck, and the resulting chaos, often accompanied by costly lawsuits. How can you get out of the toxic cycle, change it for the better, and still manage to keep your job? You can do it all by yourself—diplomatically, directly, and definitively. Read on to find out how.

Why You Need to Deal with Difficult Co-Workers Yourself

You need to deal with difficult co-workers yourself for many important reasons, including, but not limited to, the following:

- The situation is affecting *you*. It is your issue and *you* are the one who needs to deal with it, for your own benefit and sanity.
- Taking responsibility for your life, your happiness, and your work space enables you to feel you have rights.
- Handling problems yourself increases your own self-respect, raises your self-esteem, and inspires others. It gives you a sense of courage, self-empowerment, and the belief in yourself that you can effectively cope with other issues.
- When you live with a constant and chronic negative situation, your body is under siege. Stress conditions can produce physical ailments such as headaches, backaches, and digestive problems, which can worsen and become severe and debilitating.
- Handling problems yourself gives you a higher level of respect among your co-workers. It shows them that you are someone who takes the job seriously, who shows leadership abilities, and who is assertive, taking matters into his or her own hands to effectively communicate a workable solution to a challenging situation.

- Watching you as a role model can inspire others to do the same—to take the initiative to successfully confront problems themselves at work and even in their personal lives. This can lead to strong team building in other work projects besides righting wrongs.
- Standing up for yourself can inspire you to go back to school, become a manager, or pursue another career that once seemed out of reach.
- Your handling problems effectively will be noticed by members of management when they are looking to promote someone, especially to a supervisory position.
- On the other hand, if you continue to go to managers to solve your smaller problems, they will tire of you and may consider you a nuisance and a weakling. They will not regard you as management material or someone to promote. They will regard you as someone who can't be independent, strong, self-reliant, and decisive, all of which does not inspire confidence. In addition, repeated reports to the manager will turn you into "The Boy (or Girl) Who Cried Wolf," and you will lose credibility. When you really need help from a manager, they may ignore it.
- Effectively confronting issues yourself with compassion, understanding, firmness, and clarity makes the company a stronger, better place to work and creates a good example and role model for other employees.

CHAPTER 4

When Human Motives Turn Negative

Know Your Own Motives and Those of Others

First, it helps to understand *why* people do what they do so you can have more compassion for them before you decide to handle the situation directly. Having psychological knowledge, empathy, and well-developed communication skills help you to establish rapport and defuse most situations. When and if you must issue ultimatums to your co-workers about their dysfunctional conduct, these same skills and techniques will help you feel strong and assertive.

You can become an amateur psychologist by observing how other people's behavior affects you and other people in the work environment and by learning to deal directly with it in tactful yet effective ways. You don't have to have a Ph.D. and be a licensed psychotherapist to use common sense, intuition, and keen judgment in diagnosing someone's toxicity. Having this awareness, you can better understand how other people operate and what creates poisonous situations at work.

A person's motivation can stem from a variety of emotional roots. Dr. Carl Jung, a disciple of the legendary psychoanalyst Dr. Sigmund

Freud, discussed "the shadow"—the dark side of human nature. We all have a dark side, and how we deal with it makes the difference in a positive versus negative outcome. Jung advised people to make friends with their shadow by understanding that it's trying to help them to get their needs met, but in the only way it knows how—by being sneaky, self-serving, and manipulative and by doing mean, nasty, and unethical things. What Jung advised was to look deeply into our own psyches, thank the shadow for trying to help, and say no to its suggestions. Then turn it around—use positive, ethical behavior to get our needs met, which will get us on the correct spiritual and ethical path. Debbie Ford's *The Secret of the Shadow: The Power of Owning Your Story* is a powerful book that can help you deal with this issue.

So examine all of the following motivations—the general emotional categories that spur behavior. Let's take a look at the positive and negative sides of each so you can better understand your coworkers' behavior, as well as your own.

Ambition

Having goals and wanting to succeed is certainly admirable. Following and fulfilling your dreams are what life is all about. Showing the world your talents, contributing to making the planet a better place, and the pursuit of personal happiness can all work to everyone's benefit. There are also those who are ruthlessly ambitious and who will step over (or on top of) anyone else to get ahead—the Lady Macbeths of the world. They see job titles, money, and status as their divine right, and many times they do not have a solid character and the morals to achieve those goals through ethical means. They resort to manipulation, sneakiness, and whatever it takes to get ahead. They may steal your ideas or work and pass them off as their own. They may set you up for failure because it makes them look better in comparison. They may spread venomous rumors about you to destroy your reputation and credibility. Their evil knows no bounds.

Status

Some people's ambition is focused on increasing their status. Their need to "keep up with the Joneses" or have that title on their business card, move into the corner office, and get special perks emboldens them to use any means to get ahead. They are name-droppers, they have all the latest gadgets, and they dress better than most people in the office. They are shallow individuals who have little compassion for others and even less insight into their own behavior. Usually narcissistic, they believe that material possessions and whom they know are more important than the real values in life, such as love, ethics, and friendship.

Greed

Money is necessary to pay bills, get along in the world, and keep the economy going. Greed, however, is an obsession with money, and some people's ambition comes from pure greed. As seen in the movie *Wall Street*, the Gordon Gekkos of the world are motivated by their love of money, which blinds them to other people's feelings, to any spiritual awareness, to the emotional needs of their family, and to treating other people honestly and ethically. Money is their identity and goal because they mistakenly think that it will solve all their problems. Even when they are wealthy, they still feel poor and want more. Their inner poverty is insatiable, like a black hole in the universe.

Granted, money affords a certain amount of power and options, but you can't take it with you. Think of the story of King Midas, who destroyed the very thing he loved the most—his daughter—by turning her into gold. In a true-life example, Aristotle Onassis was one of the wealthiest men in the world, yet his son was killed in a tragic boating accident; he developed myasthenia gravis—a disease of the muscles and nervous system—and no doctor could cure it. Money definitely has its limitations.

Envy

Admiring what someone else has and wanting the same for yourself can serve as positive and powerful motivation. However, envious people usually feel incomplete, inadequate, and defective. They scheme how to take it from someone else by actively pursuing it, whether it's a job title, salary, or something more personal. As the Chinese proverb states, "Some people feel taller by cutting other people's heads off." They seethe just looking at other people's success and feel diminished, flawed, and bad about themselves, so they have to have the same or more to fulfill their dreams and resurrect their damaged self-image. The green-eyed monster is one of the seven deadly sins for a reason.

Fear

It's perfectly reasonable to fear snakes, poisonous spiders, or vicious dogs. On the other hand, constantly frightened people are always walking on eggshells, afraid of being fired, of making a mistake, of not being liked. Many bosses bank on this fear and use it to manipulate, control, and intimidate workers into submission. Fearful people can sell out a co-worker, betray a friend, and even lie to save themselves or their job. They are usually not emotionally strong people of principle, and in fact they can be spineless, weak, and without a moral compass. By choosing the path of least resistance based on their fear, they reveal their lack of inner strength and they might even end up selling out friends and co-workers.

Ego

Each of us may have areas of inadequacy. For those with a totally inadequate ego, their boasting, bragging, and conversational domination are fueled by their own insecurity and this is their way of being in the world—never feeling complete. They must always be "one up" on everyone else. They use various tactics to intimidate others and to assert their "uniqueness." They usually hate losing or coming in second, and they feel the constant need to be number one.

Many times, they will cheat and lie to get ahead and to win. An unchecked ego can make someone extremely competitive.

Those driven by ego will do nearly anything to get ahead, to make their quota, and to please the boss. They can be ruthless, amoral, deliberate, and devious. Read *Snakes in Suits: When Psychopaths Go to Work,* by Paul Babiak and Robert Hare for more on this toxic personality trait.

Revenge

Some people can be quite vindictive. A perceived slight from someone is all it takes to make a seemingly innocuous remark fester into a major, infectious wound. They will wait however long it takes to give payback to their "aggressor." They will plot, connive, and strategize to enact revenge and get back at anyone whom they believe has wronged them. Usually very sensitive and thin-skinned, revenge-minded people take everything personally and have little objectivity or a sense of humor about themselves and about life. They can't usually forgive and forget. They can be rigid, seeing the world in black-and-white terms, and very judgmental.

Insecurity

Most of us have insecurities, things we don't like about ourselves and hope to improve. People who are always fearful, not feeling good enough about themselves, and having low self-esteem, however, can be a constant threat and totally undependable. They can also lash out, become surly, or withdraw. They doubt their abilities, second-guess themselves and others, and try to please their superiors. They will sell out a co-worker to gain the approval of a boss or manager.

When people don't think highly of themselves, feel insecure, and have gaping black holes of neediness, it is likely that they suffer from low self-esteem. Sometimes this trait manifests itself when people strive to make themselves feel better by putting others down. Or they can be a doormat and let others take advantage of them. Either way, it's a losing game for them and for you.

Hatred

When dealing with those with hatred issues, you may not have said or done anything offensive, but you may remind them of someone they hate or exhibit a trait they dislike about themselves. Their projection makes you the target of their own anger at themselves. They have little introspection for understanding that we all have strengths and weaknesses or flaws. They refuse to take the time to love themselves and acknowledge their own humanness and frailty. Instead they take their own self-hatred and dump it in your lap and you become the target of their fury.

Obsessive Crush

Perhaps you smiled at someone who was enamored with you, or you had a working lunch with someone once, and you didn't realize this person had a crush on you. You thought he or she was just a friendly co-worker, but in reality the person may have been secretly in love with you and jealous if you're involved with someone else. Those who misinterpret a smile as sexual interest, a handshake as a caress, or a hug as a betrothal suffer from a condition known as erotomania.

The person suffering from erotomania may even have "shrines" to you—photo boards covered with pictures of you—which you never see. Perhaps he or she made an overture, and you said no as tactfully as you could, but now this person is going to get back at you because you didn't pursue the relationship. This person may spread rumors about you or post libelous items about you on the Internet. He or she may even stalk you outside of the office. Be careful. Such people can be dangerous.

Power

We all want to have a sense of power, effectiveness, and control in our lives. People who crave power above all else can be control freaks and even emotional sadists—they need to assert their influence and control over you to show you who is in charge. They want you to fear them. They attract passive, dependent personalities who want someone to tell them what to do and how to run their lives. They like to browbeat and intimidate people. If the person is your boss, you may meet with many obstacles, rules, and objections as to why you can't leave if you decide to quit or transfer to another department. Your boss may go to HR or higher levels to keep you in his or her web of control. If that's the case, you must do all you can to get away. Ask HR for help. You may even have to quit or find another department head who requests you or ask HR to transfer you.

Dependency

Many co-workers become overly attached to others in the workplace, seeking friendship, a compassionate ear, or help with assignments. Usually weak and operating from fear, low self-esteem, and ineptness, they will bond with someone by using flattery, compliments, or full-blown adoration. Many times this can turn into a sick codependency from which you may find it hard to escape because you feel pity, guilt, or a strong need to help and play rescuer. You may also love the flattery and ego strokes, but that wears thin when the dependency strangles you and makes it hard to breathe. Even bosses become dependent on their assistants and on certain employees because they make the boss look good, cover for him or her, and may know more than he or she does about the office and the business.

Approval

We all want to be acknowledged for our hard work and have approval for our competence. Some people constantly look for praise from co-workers and superiors, perhaps playing out a pattern from childhood with their parents or teachers. They seem to need acknowledgment, attention, and praise. They can be hooked to the external validation because they may have no inner confirmation system and suffer from low self-esteem. If they were able to congratulate themselves on a job well done, they would not be so needy, desperate, or weak in looking outside themselves for validation. Approval seekers can become weighty encumbrances at work. The more sadistic bosses or co-workers will deliberately withhold approval to hurt them or keep them hooked and wanting more.

Acceptance

People motivated by acceptance need to feel part of a group and can be very frightened to disagree with anyone. Perhaps there was much dissension, arguing, and possibly even domestic violence in their childhood, which they avoid as much as possible as an adult. Even when they disapprove or don't like something, they usually will put on a happy smile and agree because their fear of being rejected or criticized is so strong. They have difficulty being assertive and standing up for anything, least of all themselves. They need to belong to "the group" and they usually will do whatever it takes to avoid rocking the boat.

Although there are other motivating factors in people's behavior, these are the main ones that are crucial in understanding others. Look at which motivations propel you, and develop some insight into your own behavior. Then examine and understand what motivations drive your toxic co-workers so you can communicate effectively with them to change their toxic behavior.

This book is primarily concerned with people's toxic motivations, which get in the way of healthy, open communication. By recognizing them, understanding them, and knowing how to confront them, you can get people to change their dysfunctional behavior to make your work life a more peaceful, productive environment. Later, we will deal with each toxic type of behavior that you may encounter in a workplace. Specific lines are given to you to learn, rehearse, and say when you confront the offender at work. Use these sentences, tailor them to fit your own situation, and make them your own, so that when you do face your toxic co-workers, you will feel confident and ready to respond to whatever they may say.

CHAPTER 5

Everyone Has Positives and Negatives

Know and Accept Yours and Others'

It's important to remember that life on planet Earth is filled with duality. Everything has its opposite: liberal and conservative, young and old, male and female, rich and poor, and good and evil. Unfortunately, this is not a perfect planet and there will likely always be conflict, disagreement, and dissent. Accepting this reality helps us to cope with its challenges; and while it doesn't mean we condone or want to participate in the dark side of life, it does demand that we recognize that it exists and are willing to confront it when it affects us. Sticking our heads in the sand like an ostrich and hoping negative things or people will disappear is *not* the way to deal with life. We must have the courage to stand up to toxic people and cope with the events that adversely affect us.

As the saying goes, "The only constant is change." Dealing with change on a daily basis is a challenge. But if you have a toxic situation, just know that you can alter it. If you don't like something, you can do something about it. This book addresses negative situations and helps you to turn them into positive ones, by identifying why they are like that in the first place, what human motivations are behind the difficult behavior, and how confronting it diplomatically, honestly, and directly can change it into a workable situation. You have a choice in every situation you face: you can continue with the negativity or you can deal with it and turn it into a win/win. It's also about your perspective: is your glass half empty or half full? Your outlook and choice are always yours to create.

We must also have perspective and a sense of humor about life, to see the irony and to be able to laugh about the insanity of human behavior, our own included! Laughing generates endorphins, which are natural antidepressants that the body produces; that is much healthier than taking prescription drugs to make us happier. The saying "Comedy is tragedy plus time" tells us that what seems like disaster when it's happening can turn out to be one of the funniest stories we tell after a week or so has passed and we see the folly and absurdity of it all.

Learning and accepting these truths about how the world works is like getting the instruction booklet to a new device. It helps you to know how to operate it, to know its limitations, and to appreciate what it can and can't do, so that you can have a happier, more productive life. Being psychologically adept makes you wiser, more mature, and more savvy about confronting certain people about their toxic behavior. You can recognize the roots of their toxic behavior and know how to solve challenges they present, thereby enhancing your own life, work environment, and the lives of others. For those who really love their jobs, you may even experience the joyful anticipation of wanting to go to work in the morning. When you have found your true calling, you eagerly look forward to sharing and expressing your talents at your trade, business, or organization, relieved that toxicity is gone.

Know and Accept Your Own and Others' Positives and Negatives

One step to becoming a more effective, self-aware person is to make lists of your own positive and negative traits—what you like and don't like about yourself as a worker and as a person—and then decide what you'd like to change on that list and how you'd like to modify your behavior—what type of person you would like to become.

You can also prepare a similar list concerning others in your life—family, friends, boss, and co-workers. This exercise enables you to see that everyone, including you, has certain skills and abilities as well as flaws that you should be aware of and that you need to learn to deal with.

When you do your own self-assessment, compare it to the traits—both positive and negative—that you feel you share with others. Does someone have a trait that you despise because you can't stand the same trait in yourself? The result of this exercise is to learn self-acceptance as well as acceptance of others—to see the blessings and the deficits in yourself as well as in other people. It will help to stop being so critical of yourself when you realize that you are not perfect and neither is anyone else, regardless of whether they think so or not (and lots of people tend to think they are perfect!).

What we don't like and refuse to accept in ourselves, we don't like and refuse to accept in others. This is called "projection," and it is a defense or coping mechanism, as coined by two legendary psychoanalysts, Anna Freud and her famous father, Sigmund Freud. We take our anger at ourselves and project it onto others, transferring our flaws and negative traits over to them. But if we can see the "log in our own eye" and see why we don't like this trait in ourselves, it can give us more understanding about others. When we accept our flaws as truth, we develop compassion for others, see them as human beings with strengths and weaknesses, and appreciate that they may be doing their best under challenging circumstances. Hopefully, this will enable us to confront people about their toxic behaviors with more understanding and empathy.

We all have filters over our eyes, ears, and other senses. We all see, hear, and sense the same things differently because of our physiology, DNA, culture, upbringing, and many other factors. We need to take all of these into consideration when we decide to communicate with someone who exhibits toxic behavior. Know as much as possible about a person before you decide to confront him or her. Then, as the song says, "walk a mile in their shoes before you abuse, criticize, and accuse."

Here's an example: Let's say that your boss or co-worker is micromanaging you, and it drives you crazy. Perhaps he had a critical father or mother and was under a great deal of pressure to be perfect as a child. This boss or co-worker grew up believing that he was responsible for everything and if he made a mistake, he was "a bad person." If he didn't make mistakes and was "perfect," then he would be loved, thought of as "a good boy," or at least not yelled at or beaten. Now you can see the roots of his obsessive-compulsive nature. When you talk with him, be sure to reassure him that you respect and admire his commitment to excellence, and encourage him to relax. Assure him that you share the same commitment to excellence and that his constant "nudging" is perhaps getting in your way and interfering in your productivity. Ask for more trust from him, more flexibility, and to be left alone. Assure him that you will check in with him once in the morning, once in the afternoon, and whenever you need his feedback or a question answered. Then he will feel that he is still in control, and you will have more breathing space. Perhaps when the boss or co-worker learns to trust your dependability, he will loosen up his micromanaging style and you'll only have to check in once a day or even once a week. Now that's how to approach a toxic co-worker or boss where everyone wins!

Now review the same scenario in your own life. Do you hate being micromanaged because your mother or father did it to you? Did you feel that you weren't trusted or were thought of as dumb and not smart enough to see mistakes? How did it make you feel—inadequate, angry, and resentful? Now can you see how your micromanaging boss or co-worker feels?

Even if you didn't have such a parent, being micromanaged can be exasperating! You have the right to tell your micromanager to stop and to follow the plan outlined above so his anxiety, fear, and mistrust is allayed and you have the space to work in peace. Once again, everybody wins!

PART II

COMMUNICATION AND RELATIONSHIPS

Techniques to Get It Right

CHAPTER 6

Good Business Relationships Are Built on Trust, Honesty, and Open Communication

Trust, honesty, and open communication are the cornerstones of good business relationships and a healthy organization. Owners, managers, supervisors, and bosses need to establish a company with the values of candor, support, and empowerment for all employees. They should establish high but attainable goals, reward employees for their achievement, and acknowledge their accomplishments in all they do. Communication, collaboration, and compromise are three keys of getting along in an office; you don't want to sell out, compromise your integrity, or do something that you feel is unethical or immoral, but you want to be flexible, understanding, and see it from the other person's viewpoint. You also want to state your opinions, rights, and vision, and then reach a solution that works for everyone.

It's true that certain company plans and strategies may not need to be shared with all employees until the time is right, and a good manager will say, "I can't discuss that right now," instead of playing games or being evasive and duplicitous. If a company is engaged in high-level secrecy for the government, or it needs to guard a new design, formula, or device, then secrecy is understandable. It's *how* you state something that makes the difference. Do it diplomatically: "I'm sure you understand it is company policy that I can't discuss that, and when I can share it, I will."

Some co-workers are intrusive and nosy and even violate company rules, so you must set limits. More information on handling those types can be found in Part III.

Open, honest communication built on trust enables employees to feel secure and safe, and it provides a solid work environment that leads to higher productivity, more creativity, better cooperation, and more stable, consistent, and happier relationships between co-workers and between management and the workforce.

Suspicion, doubt, and distrust of someone's integrity or words are all dangerous to the health of a company as well as to employees' individual health. People spend too much time playing office politics and watching their backs instead of focusing on their work and the tasks at hand, all in a cooperative effort to further their own and the company's goals.

Team building is another important key to success in any company. The right chemistry among co-workers is crucial. Setting goals, timelines, and appropriate accountability are all part of project management. Discussions about personality conflicts, disagreements, and arguments must be handled tactfully, clearly, and firmly. Accountability and responsibility are two other elements of successful teams. Agreeing to disagree is important to accept and build into your expectations. Ultimately the team leader must take the initiative to guide the course and make the final decisions based on input from the team members. If there is no team leader, then the different personalities must mesh well in order for the team to be productive. When you have to work with other people in an office, you are expected to get along for the sake of the company. Politeness, respect, and honest communication are crucial and must be observed. But in order to achieve that, you will have to communicate openly, honestly, and often.

CHAPTER 7

Know and Align Your Attitude, Intentions, and Hidden Agendas

As we learned in the previous chapters, being aware of yourself and others is the first key to effective, caring communication. The next step is having the right attitude for following through with it. Being aware of where other people are coming from gives you more information as to how you should proceed. Your attitude, though, is what helps you get your point across and resolve the issues.

You must have a positive attitude in dealing with other people in the workplace. Believe that you are going to make progress in communication. If you go into a negotiation or dispute thinking negatively and assuming the worst, then many times this mind-set taints the outcome as your thoughts act as a steamroller in paving the street of your dreams or nightmares—it all depends on your outlook. Will the interaction be a success with mutual understanding and positive change or will it be an explosive failure, erupting in a screaming match and causing increased animosity?

People can sense if you initiate discussion with a phony façade, like the Smiling Cobra personality described in Chapter 29. If you lack openness and sincerity, it shows and people can sense it very quickly. You need to approach the other person from a place of genuine concern and understanding. Only then will you even have a chance of getting through to him or her.

Most people have hidden agendas—both positive and negative—when dealing with others. They aim for a raise or a promotion, they want their boss's job, or they even want *your* job. The list is endless. When you know this, you can be wary and look and listen for the signs of what they really want. You must read between the lines and attempt to discover what their hidden agendas might be. Figure out what your co-workers really mean, even if they won't tell you. "Calling a process shot" on hidden agendas is discussed in Chapter 16. This is very helpful to defuse and deflate posturing and manipulation.

If *you* have a hidden agenda, admit it to yourself. Be positive and direct about it. Using clear, honest, and direct communication is better than being sneaky, deceptive, and false. If your goal is to put the other person down, prove them wrong, or pass judgment, you will have doomed the communication from the start. If you're just giving lip service out of obligation and duty, then your intention is muddled and the result will be compromised. It is a toxic intention in itself to proceed with a confrontation bearing those attitudes. You must make an honest, open attempt at dialogue with someone to get things resolved in a positive manner.

If, on the other hand, your intention is to truly resolve the issues—and it should be—then state as much from the beginning. You may not want to become the person's BFF, but you owe it to yourself and to her or him to clear up any misperceptions and bad feelings. It may be difficult to hear mistakes you have made, to be wrongly accused of something, or to feel ashamed of or guilty for something you've done. But if all of this is to correct an error so it doesn't happen again, then it serves a good purpose.

Remember, confrontations with bosses or co-workers can very easily turn into two-way streets—you want to tell them what *they* need to work on, and they want to tell you some things *you* should work on as well. Be tactful in presenting your case, keep your emotions in check when they present theirs, and lay out the facts logically. Proceed as you would in a courtroom—each person has a chance to discuss his or her side of the case, and you must listen to what the other person is saying. Make notes to rebut when it is your turn and give clear examples. Listen quietly when others are speaking, as they should when it is your turn.

You must be open-minded, stay objective, and hear the other person's side of the story. Remember that each person—including you—has filters on his or her eyes and ears and perceptions that are colored by experience. You are the same way. Allow your co-workers to express themselves and to tell you the whole story. Let them get it all out completely before you say anything; you can make notes and ask questions when they are finished. Then it's your turn to tell your side of the story. Most people just need a place to feel completely "heard," and a good co-worker should provide an emotional atmosphere of openness, safety, and nonaccusatory questions.

CHAPTER 8

Eliminate Weasel Words and Escape Clauses

Let's look at some specific words and phrases that are used by some people to buy time, avoid giving answers, and escape commitment. If you use these words and phrases yourself, take a scalpel and cut them out of your thinking, speaking, and writing. Words like these only weaken you and make you sound noncommittal, undependable, and untrustworthy.

"Try"

Try is a weasel word. "Well, I'll try," some people say. It's a cop-out. They're just giving you lip service when they probably have no real intention of doing what you ask. Remember what Yoda says to Luke Skywalker in *Star Wars*: "Do or do not—there is no *try*." Take Yoda's advice. Give it your all when you attempt something. And if it doesn't work, start over. Put passion into your work and give it your best effort, so you can know that you did all you could to make it happen. Swing for the bleachers! So if the outcome you were expecting didn't come to fruition, it's not because you didn't do everything you could to make it happen! It just wasn't the right time for it or it wasn't meant to be.

"Whatever"

This word is a trusted favorite of people who want to dismiss you, diminish what you say, or get rid of you quickly. "Whatever," they will say as an all-purpose response to your earnest request. It's an insult and a verbal slap in the face. It's a way to respond to a person without actually responding. When you say *whatever* after another person has said his or her piece, you have essentially put up a wall between the two of you and halted any progress in communicating. It's a word to avoid.

"Maybe" and "I don't know"

People will sometimes avoid making a decision and hide behind words and phrases like "maybe" and "I don't know." There's a difference between legitimately not knowing something and using words like these as excuses. Sometimes during a confrontation people will claim not to know something or offer the noncommittal response "maybe," just to avoid being put on the spot. If that seems to be the case, ask, "When do you think you will know?" or "How can you find out?" Don't let the person off the hook so easily.

"I'll get back to you"

When people need to buy time or avoid revealing a project's status, they will say, "I'll get back to you," and they usually never do. If people say they will get back to you, always clarify. Ask them *when* they will get back to you, and make sure they specify the day and time. If they don't, then pin them down to a day and time and hold them to it. If they won't give you a day or time, tell them you'll call in a day or week and follow up. Make sure you call and get the information you need.

"If"

Projects depend on everyone doing his or her part. People who use *if* are usually playing the blame game and betting against themselves. They like to set conditions, rather than assuming a successful outcome. People who rely on conditional responses are fortifying themselves against potential failure. They will say, "If Bob finishes his part, then I can do my part." They're laying the groundwork for a "no fault" excuse and for not finishing their work. There are always alternatives, other routes, and ways to get the job done. Excuse makers usually have the energy of a slug, the vision of Mr. Magoo, and the spine of a jellyfish. You don't want them on your mountain-climbing team up K-2 or Mount Everest.

"Yes, but . . ."

This is another excuse. You might give your team members suggestions or solutions and they come back to you with "Yes, but . . ." as a response. They don't really want answers, help, or solutions. You need to call the "Yes, but . . ." people out on their avoidance tactic by saying something like: "You know, Jackie, every time I offer you a suggestion you say, 'Yes, but . . . ,' which makes me think you don't really want to solve this problem. That's not going to work. If you want to play the victim, go right ahead, but I'm not going to allow you to keep this up and I may have to report you." After a response like that, you can be assured that the next words you hear will not be "yes, but . . ."!

"I guess . . ."

This is usually said in a weak, soft-spoken, shoulder-shrugging manner. It's another attempt to shirk responsibility—a phrase is only muttered when people half agree with you, but want to leave enough leeway to say, "Well, I didn't really know. . . . I was only guessing." If you use this phrase, cut it out of your vocabulary.

"We'll see . . ."

How many times did we hear our parents say this? We knew they were buying time, avoiding a fight or confrontation, or really saying no. It's better to be decisive and honest by saying, "I need more information. Please present your case or send me the data—both pro and con—so I can make an informed decision." That way the interested parties will contribute to an in-depth, well-researched "verdict."

CHAPTER 9

Recognize and Interpret Body Language

Body language can mean any motion that someone does to communicate something nonverbally. Watch for the following behaviors and stances in yourself and in others. Make sure that what you're saying with your body language is in agreement with what you're trying to convey in conversation. I've included below some examples of body language—some of which are obvious, some that are less so—and expert interpretations on what they communicate:

Arms crossed across the chest

- "I'm closed off from hearing the message and I'm inaccessible."
- "I don't trust you so I have to protect myself."
- "I need to be convinced by facts."

Looking at a watch or the clock

- "I want this to be over soon because I have better things to do."
- "You're not important enough for me to listen to."
- "I hope you will shut up and get out of my office."

Rolling eyes

- "You are impossible!"
- "That is a stupid remark and I don't respect you."
- "That's never going to happen! Oh, right! Sure! You're in Fantasyland."

Sighing

- "I'm bored and wish this were over."
- "You're so naïve."
- "I have no patience to deal with you."

Reading the newspaper, answering e-mails, watching TV, not facing you

- "I don't want to deal with this."
- "I'm doing something else because you're not important enough to command my full attention."
- "Can't you see you're interfering with my private time?"

Tapping fingers

- "I'm marking time until you leave."
- "I'm impatient and I can't wait for this to be over."
- "I'm judging you and I'm plotting my revenge as you speak."

Poor eye contact

- "I'm guilty and I can't look you in the eye."
- "I'm lying and/or hiding something from you, so I can't face you."
- "I would rather not be having this conversation at all and if I don't look at you, I can pretend it's not real."

Lip biting

- "I'm nervous and angry."
- "I'm not going to say what I really feel because I don't feel safe telling the truth."
- "I have to hold my tongue because if I really told you what I thought of you, you'd hit me, fire me, or demote me."

Extra-strong handshake

- "I am an intimidating force to be reckoned with."
- "You can't take advantage of me."
- "I am the dominant alpha dog in all situations."

Weak handshake

- "I have no energy, creatively or physically."
- "I never commit fully to any particular task."
- "I am undependable."

Flirty behavior (lip licking, eye batting, sexy smiles, etc.)

- "I might be up for anything. Try me."
- "If you scratch my back, I'll scratch yours."
- "Please let me get my way."

Crying

- "I am a very sympathetic character."
- "Please let me off the hook."
- "Protect me."

Be sure to always watch what you say, and watch what your body is saying as well. Some books that discuss body language in more detail can be found in the Bibliography and on my website.

CHAPTER 10

Your Voice Is a Communication Tool

Volume, tone, cadence, and enunciation are all crucial in any communication. Your voice is an important communication tool and you need to use it effectively. Keep a steady cadence with appropriate pauses. Don't talk too quickly or too slowly. Talking too slowly conveys that you're a boring person or don't have much energy. You will lose people's attention as they nod off to your droning. Think of them as having a mental TV remote to click you off and see what's on another channel. You can prevent that from happening by being interesting, lively, fun, and informative. If you talk too slowly, they will also dismiss what you are saying. They won't want to talk to you and they'll work with someone else if they can.

Conversely, if you talk too fast, people may not hear everything you say. They may be too timid to ask you to repeat yourself, so you may injure your own transactions, business orders, or commissions. You may also convey that you are fast in everything you do, which may convey that you rush into things, do things too quickly, overlook certain details, and don't have good quality control. It also may impart that you can't wait to finish the conversation and leave, none of which is conducive to good business relationships with co-workers or anyone else. People may think you are trying to slip something into the conversation and pull a fast one, hoping no one will hear it, like those TV and radio ads that speed up at the end when the announcer is reading the "fine print."

Enunciate your words. Complete your *g*s at the end of gerunds (i.e., say *feeling, talking, writing*; never *feelin', talkin', writin'*.) Don't whisper. Politely ask the other person to speak up if you can't hear. When you talk, speak with conviction, crisp diction, and clarity. Work with a voice coach if necessary. Speech patterns can be revealing about your education, class, regional upbringing, and breeding. If need be, you can always go to the library and get CDs that can help you with your speech or even go to a speech coach therapist.

Shouting and screaming are, of course, always inappropriate in a work setting. These are the tactics of bullies. If you have a meek, monotonous voice, no matter what you are saying, people might perceive you to be droning on and on. A tone like this gives people the impression that you are boring and that what you have to say is dull and unimportant. You don't capture someone's attention with a monotone. Put some vitality in your voice. Take speech lessons, join your local Toastmasters club for practice, or work with a voice coach to make your voice captivating so people will want to listen to you.

Conversely, if you are soft-spoken, you put a strain on the interaction because no one can hear you. People may feel it's rude to ask you to speak up, and then your important communication can be lost. We all wish we had a voice like a radio announcer, but if that's not possible, keep it in a medium tone and volume range so that the people you are communicating with can hear you and will pay attention.

If you are on the other end of a conversation with a mumbler, be assertive and ask him or her to speak up. Remember the *Seinfeld* episode with the woman who was a mumbler? Jerry ended up wearing a "puffy shirt" on TV because he was too polite to clarify what she was saying and he didn't realize what he agreed to. She wasn't speaking clearly or loud enough, and instead of asking her to talk louder, he simply acquiesced, ended up feeling like a fool, and was humiliated on television. It was his own fault for being too shy or too reticent to ask. Don't let it happen to you.

If you have a high-pitched, nasal voice or a shrieking or screeching voice, people will want to use earplugs. It may sound like nails on a blackboard to them, and they may tend to avoid you just because of your unpleasant voice. Lower your tone, speak from your diaphragm, and just generally try to make your voice more soothing so people will want to hear you and communicate with you. When I host my radio show, I use my "radio voice" and aim for an octave lower because it's more pleasant to listen to.

Whiners and crybabies are two other groups that people don't want to listen to. Their voices are as irritating to hear as fire engine sirens in traffic. Stop the excuse machine and the sob story. Take responsibility for your part, and state what the problem is. Get to the point quickly and say what you need to say to explain exactly how the situation can be resolved. Whiners and crybabies must learn to stop their "helpless act" and become more assertive and powerful when they speak.

CHAPTER 11

Motivating Your Co-Workers to Change

Motivating co-workers to comply with your wishes can be a delicate balance of the "carrot" and the "stick." When you confront someone and describe his or her toxic behavior, be very specific. Give the time, place, and setting of what you saw and heard. Then when the person changes and does things correctly, do the same thing—tell the person how you witnessed him or her handling a situation differently and that you appreciate it. Do this every time you see a co-worker making a shift in toxic behavior. People need to have their positive growth pointed out to them because it reinforces the behavior change, and they feel rewarded and gratified to be noticed. It's an "'Attaboy!" or "'Attagirl!" that makes them want to do more.

One's sense of pride in himself or herself can make all the difference, but positive reinforcement from you is crucial. Your encouragement and compliments reinforce the changes and acknowledge the person's growth. It's a powerful tool to use as the "carrot," and most people respond to this type of reinforcement. You can't expect perfection or immediate change—sometimes people forget or backslide—so be patient.

Unfortunately, there are those who take advantage of others and who see kindness as weakness. It is not. The "stick" may need to be employed with co-workers like these, to establish limits and boundaries, indicate guidelines, and demonstrate and set performance standards, quotas, and goals. You may have to issue ultimatums if those expectations are not met. You may also need to remind them that you *will* go to the boss again or to HR if the toxic behavior isn't rectified. Fear of reprisal can often motivate people to change. They don't want to be dragged into HR or the boss's office nor do they want a bad report in their personnel file. Both the carrot and the stick are useful tools for motivation.

CHAPTER 12

Four Different Intentions of Communication

Win/Win, Win/Lose, Lose/Win, and Lose/Lose

The intentions of interpersonal communications are crucial to their outcome. Be aware of your conscious and unconscious intent. The intentions can be simplistically divided into four types of situations:

- win/win
- win/lose
- lose/win
- lose/lose

Try to identify your own intentions when you talk to someone. Read the following example descriptions of the kinds of intention conveyed by each type of communication and see which one fits you:

Win/Win

"I intend to be honest, direct, open, and clear. I want both of us to come out of this encounter as winners. I want you to be happy and get your needs met, and I want to do the same. I'll empower you and I hope you'll do the same for me. That way we will be happy, satisfied, and productive. We will be able to work together again with no hard feelings. We can agree to disagree. We may have to be flexible, give a little something, and compromise to coexist peacefully, and I'm willing to do that to achieve a win/win solution."

Win/Lose

"I want to win and I want you to lose. I will do everything I can to make sure I will win and you will lose. I have to feel good about myself and that is at your expense and involves your losing, so that I am the victor and the conqueror. I don't care about you or the outcome. I have to have all my needs met while meeting none of yours. I'm really not even listening to you. I may even go through the motions to look like I care, but I don't. It's all about me, not you."

Lose/Win

"I'm a victim; I will look vindicated by losing and making you out to be the winner, the brute, and the conqueror, while I play the powerless, whining, helpless victim. You may win, but you will appear to be a cruel bully to others. I enjoy being a doormat so that others will feel sorry for me. I set it up this way so that you will appear selfish and mean. Inwardly, I love losing because that way my needs are met and in a way, I win. I make myself the victim because I really don't think I deserve anything better. I'm also afraid of arguing and I don't know how to compromise. I'm terrified of my own positive power and of being someone's equal, so I'll use my power in a negative way to look like the helpless, put-upon victim."

Lose/Lose

"I am so angry, hateful, and self-destructive that I want to lose and have you lose as well. I'll do everything I can to be a victim and to bring you down with me. I will look like a helpless victim and get sympathy from people, and I'll also bring you down, too, because I have never learned to use my power constructively. I only know how to make things difficult for both parties by being angry, mean-spirited, and vicious."

It's obvious that the best interaction is the one motivated by win/win ideology. This way all parties walk away with their egos intact, a sense of goodwill, and a renewed sense of power as well as getting all or most of what they want. If you feel you have a pessimistic, destructive outlook and negative personality, and if you sincerely desire to change it, then get into therapy and read books about how to overcome it and see your glass half full instead of always half empty. My website contains bibliographies to help you. The self-help section in bookstores or online book companies can help you find such material.

Solid communication can prevent arguments, misery, and destruction, and that is what we must aim for. Win/win communication takes a great deal of maturity, patience, and commitment to work out the issue at hand. There are always solutions. You can agree to disagree—two people don't always have to see eye to eye on every issue. Commit to the possibility of everyone getting his or her way, working together successfully, and communicating openly and honestly. You can do that through win/win communication.

CHAPTER 13

Four Types of Behavior

Assertive, Aggressive, Passive-Aggressive, and Passive

There are basically four types of behavior in terms of temperament and energy:

- assertive
- aggressive
- passive-aggressive
- passive

Each one can be effective in its own right, and each one has a negative side, too. These types of behavior are described in the following sections.

Assertive

In a marriage or a working relationship, it's important that you communicate with respect and equality. You want to clearly present your needs and wants and to listen to what the other person has to say. You can strive to be open and flexible in hearing the other person and what he or she needs and wants, as you hope that person is in hearing what you need and want. You want to come to an equitable and fair resolution. In this manner, you can end up finding others who can cooperate and figure out situations where everyone benefits and thrives. The negative aspect of assertive behavior occurs during the times you really should be passive and not speak up.

Aggressive

Caring little for another's rights, you make sure that everything you want is accomplished, no matter what the means are to achieving this outcome, even if it includes stepping on other people's feelings, using people, and carelessly discarding them when they have served your needs. An example of positive aggressive behavior in communication, on the other hand, is confidently standing up for and supporting a colleague who was faltering in his or her response during a quarterly review meeting, perhaps even interrupting a superior. You need to do what you know is right.

Passive-Aggressive

Passive-aggressive people do aggressive things in a passive manner. They can be sneaky, underhanded, or deceitful and may do unethical and illegal things. "Forgetting" or saying you "didn't know" are two ways to cover one's tracks or minimize the deliberate or unconscious viciousness of one's behavior. Passive-aggressives may also attempt to convey the appearance of innocence or naiveté. It can be negative, spiteful behavior and used as payback, such as "forgetting" to pick up something crucial that someone needed or purposefully obstructing to prevent something from happening. People with this personality can also give you the cold shoulder, refusing to speak with you, and it can go on for days or even weeks, shutting you out of any conversation, not inviting you to meetings, and ignoring your requests. An excellent book on this topic is *Living with the Passive Aggressive Man*, by Scott Wetzler, Ph.D.

Passive-aggressive behavior has been used in a strong and positive way in the past—such as with sit-ins or passive resistance—but in an office setting, it reeks of immaturity, hidden anger, revenge, and pettiness.

Passive

Letting someone take charge, giving up your power, and acquiescing to someone else's needs are all ways that someone who is passive can come across as a doormat and a perpetual victim. The signal that passive people send out with this communication style is that they have relinquished the driver's seat of their own life. An example of positive passivity would be allowing yourself to be humiliated verbally by a co-worker or boss in front of other employees when you know what is being said is false, rather than dignifying their words with a response. Then when the truth comes out, the other person looks like a fool. But why set it up like that when you can be proactive, defend yourself, and stand up for the truth? Granted, some people are not leaders, nor do they want to be. But if passivity is creating problems in your life and you're feeling victimized, then it's time to change it. Get into therapy, read books about assertiveness, and take assertiveness training courses to develop strength, clarity, and decisiveness.

The reason for going over these behavior types is to help you become aware of how you can move from one modality to another to get your point across when dealing with a difficult co-worker, and also for you to be aware of your own types of behavior in different circumstances. To use a musical analogy, using these different types of behavior helps you play with all eighty-eight keys on the piano instead of just playing "Chopsticks" with a few selected notes. When you have identified your own communication style and that of the person you wish to confront, you will be able to adjust appropriately for clear and open communication.

CHAPTER 14

Preparation for Effective Discussion

Visualization, Intention, and Rehearsal

Visualization: The Power to Manifest Positive Results

Before you begin to approach someone, take time out to visualize the results. Focus on the win/win outcome that was described in Chapter 12. Lie down in a quiet place—preferably at home in a comfortable chair, on the sofa, or on your bed—close your eyes, and visualize what you consider the optimal outcome of the interaction to be. Run it through your brain like a movie. Watch yourself communicating, listening, and talking with the person in question. Observe yourself resolving the difference of opinion, getting your needs met, and making sure that the other person accomplishes the same thing. These positive thoughts can program your interaction and set the stage for a solid, satisfactory outcome. Get rid of any pessimistic, hopeless energy that you have. Reject the loser vibe that sets you up for defeat. Read some of the books and literature on the power of visualization that are listed in the Bibliography. Any great invention, project, or discovery came into creation because it existed as an idea—a visualized thought form—first.

Computers, the polio vaccine, airplanes—everything—began as a thought, a possibility, a concept in someone's mind first. Then the "how-to" began—the sketches, the variables, the testing, the laboratory experiments, the conclusions, and the retesting. So when you are approaching a difficult, even scary, encounter with someone, see it in your mind first and run it through your inner movie screen again and again, so that you can feel comfortable and at ease when talking to the targeted person. Thoughts are invisible forms of energy, and they are the first step in creation in art, music, science, mathematics, and everything else. So align your thoughts in a positive way to a calm, productive outcome where everyone wins.

Intention: Stay Clear in Win/Win Communication

We reviewed win/win communication in Chapter 12. Now you must have the clear intention that you want your discussion with your co-worker to be a win/win and you need to stay in that frame of mind. You want your toxic co-worker to stop the annoying, dangerous, or distracting behavior, and you would also like him to win in a way that he learns from it and will not do it to you or to other people again. If there is something that you are doing that bugs him, you want to be open to hearing it so that you can change it yourself. Just as your efforts to correct this can take 100 percent of your energy, your efforts also need to be 100 percent aligned with your visualization and intention. Read books and listen to CDs on intention, such as those by Wayne Dyer, Claude Bristol, Napoleon Hill, Norman Vincent Peale, and others, which are listed in the Bibliography and on my website.

Rehearsal: Practice What to Say and Feel Comfortable

Rehearse your possibilities in front of a mirror or with a friend. Ask your friend for feedback. You may even want to audio- or videotape yourself so you can hear and see how you sound and what you look like. Critique your performance. Do it again until you feel comfortable—like a member of the debate team, an actor learning lines, or a politician giving a speech. Your effectiveness as a speaker is in the ideas you want to impart, the substance of the text, and the delivery. Know what words to stress and where to place emphasis, and believe in your statements. When you are familiar with the words, you will feel more confident.

Rehearsal is very important to success because it makes you comfortable and therefore more likely to provoke a win/win outcome. Avoid sounding canned, stilted, or phony. Put your heart and feelings into it, so that the person you are confronting can tell that you are coming from a place of genuine emotion and truth. Don't be a ham, be overly emotional, or "milk it." Rehearse what you have to say; be familiar with your text and have what you want to say down pat so that you won't be thrown off track, dissuaded from the topic, or intimidated into giving up.

CHAPTER 15

Speaking and Writing, Two Vital Keys to Communication

The essence of this component of effective communication is threefold: honesty, clarity, and brevity. You can start the interaction in person speaking directly to your toxic co-worker or you can put it in writing via a letter or an e-mail. The choice is up to you. Some people like to do both. The important thing to remember is to be truthful, perfectly clear, and concise so that the person you are confronting gets the message but doesn't feel insulted, overwhelmed, or confused.

Consider writing out exactly what you want to say for yourself *before* you make your first in-person contact with the person you are confronting. Make bullet points to remind yourself of your agenda. Put them on a note card and carry it with you, if need be. Doing so will assist you if you get nervous or forget what you wanted to talk about. Even one-word cues on a file card may be enough to help you remember everything you planned to say, but if you feel you need full sentences, then write them out. Remember to include everything so that you don't have to go back to the person later and say, "Oh, I forgot to tell you . . ." Doing so dilutes your effectiveness, so be succinct and complete everything you need to say in your initial communication.

You may want to send your toxic co-worker an e-mail *before* you see him or her in person so that you can agree to a time and a place that won't be interrupted. Similarly, be sure to tell the person you are confronting that you do not wish to be interrupted until you finish saying everything you need to say. Let her know that you will give her an adequate chance to respond after you're done, and offer her some paper and a pen to make notes if she needs to. Turn off your cell phone and ask her to please do the same.

Confronting people may be very difficult for you. At first, your heart may race, your mouth may go dry, and you may even stammer, but just say what you have to say and get it done with. Know that you have a right to stop rude, caustic, and obnoxious behavior that is interfering with your work, sanity, and productivity. The next time will be easier and you'll be more confident. You may want to schedule a second or even third meeting if you can't reach agreement in one meeting. Use the same steps and have an agenda for each meeting, moving the discussion along toward closure in a win/win communication.

The more you understand the psychology behind others' toxic behavior, the more understanding you will have of how to communicate with them, how to get them to communicate with you, and how to get them to change. You will know the best ways to reach them, how they will respond, and what to say. If you are verbally attacked, you will be able to defend yourself, make your point, and be assertive. You will be able to think on your feet with the precise comeback or retort when they defend themselves or get nasty. The more you rehearse what you want to say, the more self-confident you will feel when confronting difficult people. The more you assert yourself, the easier it becomes.

You may even feel like a mediator or psychotherapist. You can develop ease and succinctness so you can politely, firmly, and clearly address any and all toxic behavior around you. And you may become an admirable role model for your co-workers to confront other obnoxious people and to stand up for themselves. You may gain so much respect in the office or at your workplace that you may even be named a supervisor or manager, get another promotion, or be rewarded with a raise. Who knows what's in store?

And if things don't change with your toxic co-worker, you may be emboldened to go to HR or higher to correct the situation. If that doesn't change things, then you have other methods at your disposal, which are addressed in Chapter 38.

Once it comes to the actual discussion or confrontation, be sure to state your purpose clearly and briefly in a sentence or two: "I'd like to talk to you about our communication and your management style, which I find is getting in the way of my productivity." Give specific examples of the behavior you are upset about, with date, time, and place if possible to illustrate your point. Tell the person how it makes you feel, then offer a solution that would work for both you and the other person. People's attention spans are short and hearing negative feedback might not be easy for them to digest at first, so say what you have to say concisely.

Some people prefer to write their entire communication in a letter or e-mail *first*. If you feel shy or nervous, perhaps that is a more effective technique for you to do *before* you speak to someone in person. It's important to know that anything you write will probably be sent to the HR director or your supervisor if you have to take your problem to a higher level, and it may end up in your personnel file, so be very diplomatic and choose your words carefully. People can't hear your tone or see your face when you send a letter or e-mail, and the written word may misconstrue your intentions. On the other hand, it is more effective for some people because you can outline your complaints rationally and in a logical order without hearing someone get defensive.

Sometimes a letter or e-mail works better as a follow-up communication after talking in person to your co-worker. The follow-up letter or e-mail should read something like this:

> Dear Kathryn,
>
> Thank you for talking with me today concerning how I feel when you interrupt my work with your personal stories. We all have work to do and when I'm on a deadline, I need to concentrate on getting my assignments done. As we discussed, you said that you will refrain from talking to me about your personal problems. I recommended that you use the EAP or our insurance carrier to pay for individual sessions of counseling if you absolutely need someone to talk to. You said you would look into

both of those options. I hope that you will keep your word on this because others in the department depend on my reports being in on time and I need to concentrate without interruptions. Thank you so much, Kathryn. I appreciate your cooperation on this.

Sincerely,

Jane Smith

You may also want to document this communication by copying (or blind-copying) your supervisor on the e-mail. The letter may go to your boss or the HR director, so it's better that it come from you. Writing this letter will cap off your efforts as you wait and see whether the other person holds up his or her end of the bargain.

CHAPTER 16

Active Listening, Paraphrasing, Calling a Process Shot, and Agreeing to Disagree

Another component of effective communication is active listening, a term coined by the late legendary psychologist Dr. Carl Rogers, founder of client-centered therapy. Active listening includes paraphrasing what you hear someone saying to you to clarify the meaning, build rapport and understanding, and discuss what is *not* being said. Your paraphrasing statement may contain compassionate words to establish empathy and to show the person you understand how he or she feels and what the person is going through. Let the person respond so that the two of you can get a dialogue going. Then after the dialogue, both parties can agree on the substance of the discussion and reach a resolution much more quickly.

Paraphrasing what someone has just said conveys to the other person that you "got" what he or she said—and what the person *didn't* say—reading between the lines to understand the emotional message as well. It helps to have agreement on the basic communication before you proceed. Make sure that what you heard is what the person said and intended. You may add your own interpretation at the end if you like before defending or rebutting the statements. The act of resolving differences should proceed like a courtroom—each person gets to present his or her side, listen to each other, then rebut with debate, dialogue, a statement of resolution, and a confirmation of future interactions.

Positive Active Listening

In a given situation, a positive active listening scenario would go something like this:

Co-Worker 1: *I'm sorry I was ten minutes late this morning. I had to pack the kids' lunches, drop them off at school, then sit in traffic because of a car accident, and there were no free parking spaces when I finally got here.*

Co-Worker 2: *Thanks for apologizing for and explaining your lateness. It sounds like you had a stressful morning and yet you still managed to get here. You've got a lot on your plate being a single mom. Is there anything I can do to help make sure you're on time from now on?*

Result: Co-worker 1 will probably feel emotionally supported and will be grateful to co-worker 2 for the empathy. There will be a better chance of teamwork, mutual support, and cooperation after such an encounter. When you offer a supportive ear after someone is late, you empower that person to be a better, more prompt worker. He or she will appreciate you for it and will help you out when you need a hand!

Negative Active Listening

Here is the same situation played out with negative and nonactive listening:

Co-Worker 1: *I'm sorry I was ten minutes late this morning. I had to pack the kids' lunches, drop them off at school, then sit in traffic because of a car accident, and there were no free parking spaces when I finally got here.*

Co-Worker 2: *Those sound like excuses to me. Everybody else somehow managed to make it here on time today with whatever they have going on in their lives. Get up earlier and plan better because you have to be here on time.*

Result: Co-worker 1 will probably feel frustration and a lack of support, in addition to the stress that comes along with being late. He or she may also experience humiliation and shame. An outcome like this one can undermine teamwork and camaraderie. It can also create a climate of resentment, revenge, and passive-aggressive behavior, with them "waiting in the bushes" to get back at you. Active listening, compassion, and clarity are always better.

Dialogue

After an active listening response of compassion and clarity, now you can have a dialogue with the person. You will have someone who is calm and open to your suggestions instead of someone who is on the defensive, disliking and mistrusting you, and suspecting your motives. What's the better emotional environment for having a dialogue? Obviously the former.

Let's say that you have a co-worker who is intrusive and always interrupts you when you're on the phone. After you've given him feedback about this problem, he may become angry, so allow him a chance to vent and to respond. Let him blow off steam and get everything off his chest. You may want to jot down some notes on what you want to say to respond. He may try to change the subject and accuse you of things that he doesn't like about you, such as how you decorate your cubicle. When it's your turn to talk, say, "I hear you're offended by how I decorate my cubicle. I'll be happy to talk about that after we deal with your intrusive behavior first." Acknowledge what he's saying, but finish first things first.

When you confront people and address an issue, most people get very defensive. Nobody likes to be confronted about his or her behavior. One of the most common immediate responses in a situation like this one is to attack the person who initiated the confrontation: "Well, *you* do this and *you* do that." I call that "The Boomerang Defense"—you're discussing *their* toxic behavior, but it comes back and lands in your lap. Don't fall for this trick. Distraction and diversion are tactics people use to avoid dealing with their own issues. Don't let them get away with it. Say, "We're talking about *your* issue of interrupting people, not how I may interrupt people." I have termed this tactic "calling a process shot."

Calling a Process Shot and Unveiling Hidden Agendas

Lots of people have hidden agendas—both positive and negative—when dealing with others. (You might have one, too, without even realizing it.) When you know this, you can be wary and look for the signs of what someone *really* wants. You must read between the lines. This is why "calling process" is a crucial element of interpersonal communication because it empowers you to "call the shot" about what is really going on. It's like a referee in a basketball or football game calling fouls—describing what is going on in the "process of the communication" and what is wrong. Calling process means telling the truth about what you are sensing—and tactfully doing so empowers you to get to the real issues faster so you can work toward a solution. Because a lot of people have hidden agendas, it's important to understand the effectiveness of calling a process shot on their secret motivations, which means cutting to the heart of the matter, beneath the frozen smiles, the polite conversation, and the thinly veiled manipulations. This is one of the best tools you can use to communicate effectively.

You can call a process shot on anyone when you begin the statement with, "It feels to me that what you're really saying is . . ." or "I think what is really going on is . . ." or "My intuition tells me that . . ."—anything that gets the point across that you are sensing more than what is being said. You can be tactful and diplomatic while still being direct as long as you own your feelings and perceptions and state what you believe. Then the person realizes that you are on to his or her game. You know the hidden agenda and how the person may be trying to snow you and you've told him or her exactly that. It puts you back in the power seat and the person you are confronting will think twice before trying to con you again. So calling process is a powerful communication tool that anyone can use easily and quickly. Trust your intuition and your gut, use common sense and tactfulness, and be direct. They will have more respect for you knowing that you're "hip to their tricks."

Resolution

The positive outcome and the purpose of any dialogue is a resolution that works for both parties. This depends on what is at stake, and whether clear, honest communication is used. Many times, a coworker has unrealistic expectations of fellow workers. Clarify what that person needs and expects and be clear on whether you can meet his or her expectations (if meeting it is what's in your best interest). State *your* needs and expectations as well. Plan to work together to meet each other's needs for a cooperative work environment so that projects can be completed and deadlines met. That sets the tone for a well-run and optimally functioning department. Remember that things change, so alter your plans and agreements accordingly. Some people only cooperate when they know they have to, but at least they are still cooperating. You can agree to disagree and still get along.

Agree to Disagree

There may be some issues that two people will never agree on. When that happens, you can agree to disagree. Respect and decency can still be maintained. Tact, social graces, and civility can all still remain in the mix. It's OK if someone disagrees with you. You don't have to win someone over to your side, and you can learn to live with dissent. It doesn't make you wrong, stupid, or old-fashioned. Republicans can be friends with Democrats, and dog lovers can get along with cat people. Both groups just see things differently because of their philosophy, life experience, and values.

This is a planet of polarity, so opposites are automatically set up by the very energy on this planet. Keep that in mind when you debate with people. Respect their views and understand why they feel the way they do—their background, culture, and all the experiences that shaped their personality. Remember, it's the little grain of sand in an oyster that makes a pearl, so a tiny irritation can produce an object of great beauty and value. Listen to opposing viewpoints. Learn why people feel and believe the way they do. Ask them questions. People sometimes change their minds when they have new information that they didn't have before and also when they come to see that their views and experiences have changed. Agreeing to disagree can eliminate tension, anger, and rage, and it allows for mutual respect and peaceful coexistence.

CHAPTER 17

"The Sandwich"

Giving Difficult Feedback with Care

Giving negative feedback to someone may not be a walk in the park, but showing sincere compassion and understanding when doing it is crucial to your success. By practicing and using the Sandwich Technique, you can achieve the outcome you're looking for. It's called the "Sandwich" because it involves couching the feedback between a positive initial compliment and a hopeful, optimistic close. I call it *feedback* rather than criticism because the word *feedback* doesn't have a pejorative connotation like *criticism* does. Feedback means you're simply telling someone how you feel and what you've observed and experienced.

Start on a cheery, complimentary note, giving the person positive feedback about what he's doing right, why he is important to the company, why you enjoy his work, and anything else you'd like to say, and then state that you'd like to resolve a few issues that have been bothering you. Give your feedback in clear, concise terms. Finally, finish with a positive and inclusive statement about how you hope that positive change will follow and that you look forward to working together.

After you have given your compliments, in two or three short sentences, state exactly the problem that you would like to resolve.

Tell the person how you feel about the toxic behavior that has been bothering you. Keep the feedback short, direct, and complete. End positively with a statement about what she's doing right and why you enjoy working with her. Make sure you close with a positive, hopeful comment, letting the person know that you intend for the situation to be resolved quickly and amiably and that you are available to dialogue about it now.

When you transition from positive compliment to feedback, be careful to use the word *and*, and do not use the word *but*. When people hear the word *but*, they feel as though they're waiting for the other shoe to drop, and they begin discounting all the nice things that have just been said. To avoid this, give the compliment and then shift over to the feedback in another sentence, using the word *and*, which makes *both* parts of the sentence true without using the word *but*. Be specific about what needs to be corrected, give examples as well as dates and times if possible, and do not disclose anyone's name who may have talked to you about it. The first conversation should simply be bringing it to your co-worker's attention.

Allow sufficient time to do this! Do not give feedback and then walk away or act as though you're in a hurry. Most people want to discuss what you've approached them about right away, and you owe it to them to make the time for it. When you approach someone with feedback, be sure you have time to discuss it after you have said your piece. If you don't have time to finish your discussion, then agree on and set a time for tomorrow or the next day to continue.

After all of the discussions are complete and you've given the person ways to improve, tell the person you would like to schedule a time to review progress; that way the person will know you mean business and are going to be observing and tracking the changes he or she makes. Let the person know that you're serious and that you want both of you to "win." State clearly that if the changes aren't made, you will be forced to go to your boss and possibly to HR to get compliance and that you hope that won't be necessary. End on a positive note, stressing the person's good points, why you like working with him or her and that you look forward to working together in the future.

Examples of Using the Sandwich Technique

First, since you probably already know what your co-worker does that is annoying, make a brief list of his or her good points. When you approach the person, do it during lunchtime or a break or at a time the two of you have previously arranged, so that it's not directly interfering with his or her workload. Ask for fifteen minutes to discuss something and do it in your office, a conference room, or someplace private. The conversation should go something like these examples.

Initial Attempt

Harry: *Hi, Bob! I enjoy working with you. Your sense of humor is always so much fun to listen to. Say, I've been wanting to mention this to you: your reports haven't been getting to me on time and it really slows me down in meeting my deadlines. Do you need some extra help? Is there anything I can do? I would really like you to have them on my desk by Wednesday at noon so I can add my part and get them to Larry by Friday. Do you think you can do that? You do? Thanks, I sure appreciate it.*

If the situation still does not improve, then schedule another chat with your co-worker. Again start out positive. Don't jump right in and tell him that he didn't correct the problem yet. Use the passive tense to remind him of what he didn't do, and urge him to change his ways.

Attempt 2

Harry: *Hi, Bob! Thanks for telling me about that magazine article. It really helped my research. By the way, I've noticed that since the last time we talked, nothing has really changed. Your reports still haven't gotten to my desk by Wednesday at noon like you promised. Why is that? What can I do to help you meet the deadline?*

Let your co-worker tell you what has kept him from doing what was promised. It may be family demands, health issues, procrastination, or a combination of all three or more. Be empathetic and practice active listening. You can either give the person more time, or you can tell him that since you gave him a warning and the situation still didn't improve, you must take action now by going to your supervisor. If nothing improves, you may need to go to HR and file a report. Let HR handle a disruptive or recalcitrant co-worker if you haven't seen sufficient change after communicating with him. Here's how it can sound as you give the warning about going to your boss or to HR:

Attempt 3

Harry: *Bob, I've spoken to you and given you several warnings about getting your work done on time and nothing has changed. If you came to me, I could have helped you get caught up. Now, I may have to go to HR and issue a formal complaint. I can't have you continue turning your work in late like this. It's affecting me and the entire department. I want to understand what is wrong, and it's difficult when you don't communicate with me. You leave me no choice but to go to HR.*

When you go to your HR representative, give the history of how you handled it before taking it to him or her so your representative knows you have made an effort to remedy the situation yourself. Here's how it should sound:

HR Conversation

Harry: *Shawna, I've talked to Bob and given him several warnings about getting his reports to me on time, including phone calls, in-person meetings, and e-mails; here's the list of my warnings. And it hasn't improved. I told him that if it still didn't change, I'd have to go to you about it. Even after that warning, nothing changed—the reports were still late and it was affecting me and the entire department. I really need you to do something about it. Thanks so much. I really appreciate it.*

In the next section, I offer some assertive techniques you can use to affect change in your co-workers. Follow the format, similar to the structure of a courtroom, so everyone is heard and all feelings and facts are explained. You should use the Sandwich Technique to open up the dialogue with a co-worker on a positive note so that the communication gets off to a good start.

Positive and Negative Outcomes

When you confront a co-worker about toxic behavior, you will get either a positive or a negative response or they will blow you off. Below are some examples to show how to respond professionally and to get your co-worker to comply. If the feedback is well received, you will have responses from your co-worker along the lines of: "You're right and I'll make it a point to improve." If the feedback is not well received, the response will sound more like this: "Leave me alone—it's none of your business. Get off my back or I'll report you for harassment!"

Positive Co-Worker 1 and Positive Co-Worker 2

Co-Worker 1: *Sally, I'm happy you work here, and I enjoy reading your reports. They are usually clear, well written, and on time. I've also noticed that you've been late to work often and that you've been taking two-hour lunches. This throws off the work schedule for me and everyone here because we're waiting for your work. I'm sure you are aware of the rules, and I hope you will respect them and continue working here because we all like having you in this department. We want you to stay because you're a valued employee. We just need you to be on time coming back from lunch, because other workers feel resentment. If you need more time during lunch for errands or emergencies, please tell your supervisor and make up the time by coming in earlier or staying later. Is there anything you need from me or from the company to make that happen? Please tell me what you need to get your work done, get your errands done during lunch, and be back at 1:00 P.M. for work because you're a valued employee. Is there anything you'd like to say about this?*

Sally: *I'm sorry I've been late. I've spent my lunch hours running over to my mother's house. She's been having some difficulty lately and I have to serve her lunch and do some errands for her. I guess I could probably take some work home or come in on weekends to make up the time. I can't come in any earlier because I have to get the kids off to school before I come in here.*

Co-Worker 1: *I didn't know all your added responsibilities with your mother and I understand. I'm sure you can take some of your reports home and bring them back the next morning. Also, you should probably tell your supervisor* *about your situation, so nobody thinks you're out getting a manicure or shopping. Thank you for telling me all of this. Shall we bring in your supervisor?*

Sally: *Yes, I'd like to tell her, and I'd like to bring work home at night so I can meet my deadlines. Thank you for understanding.*

Results: Everyone's feelings, needs, and circumstances were voiced and heard. Then a solution and a plan were offered and it looks like it could work out to everyone's satisfaction. This is an example where everything went well. Here is an example where things do not go so well.

Negative Co-Worker 1 and Negative Co-Worker 2

Co-Worker 1: *You're taking two-hour lunches and you're going to be fired if you do it again. It's bad when other employees see it. They're angry at you. You know that you're only supposed to take one hour for lunch. Now make sure that you're on time from now on or I'm going to report you to our boss!*

Sally: *Just leave me alone! I've worked hard for this company for years and if I take a little extra time at lunch, it's my business. I always get my work done.*

Co-Worker 1: *Your work is suffering and others have complained. If you're late one more time coming back from lunch, I'm telling our boss. You aren't exempt from the rules!*

Results: Co-Worker 1 took no time to use the Sandwich. He didn't stress all of Sally's good points, accomplishments, and skills. He criticized her without ever asking whether there was anything going on in her life that was adding stress or that was causing her to take longer lunch hours. A valued employee who has been trying to juggle her responsibilities—not just missing work because of laziness—may be hesitant to disclose personal information. A co-worker like that just needs a bit of understanding.

Here's another example of how being negative can alter the outcome:

Positive Co-Worker 1 and Negative Co-Worker 2

Co-Worker 1: *Sally, I'm happy you work here, and I enjoy reading your reports. They are usually clear, well written, and on time. I've also noticed that you've been late to work often and that you've been taking two-hour lunches. This throws off the work schedule for me and everyone here because we're waiting for your work. I'm sure you are aware of the rules, and I hope you will respect them and continue working here because we all like having you in this department. We want you to stay because you're a valued employee. We just need you to be on time coming back from lunch, because other workers feel resentment. If you need more time during lunch for errands or emergencies, please tell your supervisor and make up the time by coming in earlier or staying later. Is there anything you need from me or from the company to make that happen? Please tell me what you need to get your work done, get your errands done during lunch, and be back at 1:00 P.M. for work because you're a valued employee. Is there anything you'd like to say about this?*

Sally: *That's really none of your business.*

Co-Worker 1: *I sense that you're protecting your privacy and you sound like you don't trust me. Sally, I'm here to help you and to keep you meeting your workload and deadlines. If that doesn't continue, your job will no doubt be in jeopardy. You've done an excellent job all these years and I'm curious if you have other distractions like family or health issues that I might assist you with. I'd like to talk about this.*

Sally: *Stop trying to look like you care when you really don't. You're just going to tell a supervisor to write something negative in my personnel file.*

Co-Worker 1: *I hear that you're feeling defensive and that you don't want to talk about your personal problems. I'm here to help you, though, and make your life easier if I can. Whatever you're going through sounds stressful. You can talk to me about it, if you want, and it will be completely confidential. I'm not going to talk about it with others. What's going on?*

Results: Co-worker 1 took time to use the Sandwich in opening the conversation. Sally's good points, accomplishments, and skills must be repeated to her so she knows she is valued and that her co-worker is sincere and cares about her. Stress and financial problems can contribute to Sally's distrust and irritability. Co-worker 1 had to overcome Sally's paranoia, distrust, and stress by constantly repeating the care, concern, and confidentiality of his intent. Co-worker 1 did not take Sally's nasty remarks personally and instead reassured Sally that he was on her side by asking probing questions without being too intrusive. At the end of the conversation perhaps Co-worker 1 needs to give Sally some space and reschedule with her for another day.

Finally, let's observe what happens when the person who is confronting the co-worker who has been exhibiting toxic behaviors does so in a negative fashion.

Negative Co-Worker 1 and Positive Co-Worker 2

Co-Worker 1: *It's not fair that you've been late coming back from lunch for five straight days and you never get written up. Why not? If I'm late, I have to make up the hours or my pay is docked. So how do you get off so easy?*
Sally: *My mother is now a widow and she needs more help from me lately. I have to spend my lunch hour taking care of her. I need the extra time. I'll do whatever I can to make up the time.*
Co-Worker 1: *I don't care about your personal problems. Everyone is supposed to get here on time, take an hour for lunch, and get his or her work done. You should, too!*
Sally: *She needs me to feed her lunch. She has no one but me. My brother and sister live a thousand miles away.*
Co-Worker 1: *That's really not my problem, now is it?*
Sally: *I can take work home at night or I could come in on weekends.*
Co-Worker 1: *I don't know if you can come in on weekends or take work home. Get your work done here or I'm going to report you!*

Results: Co-worker 1 didn't use active listening and was cold, insulting, negative, and not understanding to an employee that did everything to convey the pressure she was experiencing. Sally gave options to make up the time and yet she was rejected. A valued co-worker was verbally abused and badly treated. Co-worker 1 criticized her without ever asking if there was anything going on in her life that was adding stress or that was causing her to take longer lunch hours. Even after Sally revealed that she was caring for her sick mother, co-worker 1 still acted without compassion. In this instance co-worker 1 is the toxic element, and Sally will need to go to someone else to resolve her problem.

In comparing all four of these interactions, you can see how easily a touchy problem can escalate into an irrevocably damaged situation, resulting in a lawsuit, a report to the Equal Employment Opportunity Commission, or a letter to the union. There is no need for this to happen. Giving negative feedback to someone may not be a cakewalk, but showing sincere compassion and understanding is crucial, and it's simple to do with the Sandwich Technique. Start out positively, then get to the feedback, and end positively. Be specific.

CHAPTER 18

Forewarned Is Forearmed

Best Scenario to Worst Scenario

When I'm doing business consultation and working with employees who are having difficulty, I always ask them three major questions:

- What could be the best possible outcome?
- What could be the worst outcome?
- What could all the possibilities in between be?

These questions allow my clients to brainstorm all of the different variations of what could happen. Then they can begin to protect themselves, by preparing for any possible outcome from Best Scenario all the way to Worst Scenario—all the good things and all the negative things that could occur. As the saying goes, "Forewarned is forearmed." Preparation for disaster and knowing the option gives people more confidence that they have a Plan B, a Plan C, and so on, all the way to Plan Z. I always push my clients to think of even better and even worse outcomes than they can imagine, just to have them aware of *everything* possible. Remember, this is not meant to be a self-fulfilling prophecy; it is preparation like strategy sessions in a war: "If the enemy moves here, then we can move here and here. . . ."

When you expect one outcome and then reality delivers another, you may feel shocked, surprised, and unprepared, as well as disappointed, angry, and sad. When that happens, your thinking can be clouded by emotion, you may sound irrational or illogical, and the interaction with co-workers or bosses can become ineffectual, heated, or diluted. You lose power, effectiveness, and credibility. When you can make lists of the possibilities and be prepared for each one of the outcomes, you will feel more confident and ready for anything.

Many people are either frozen in fear, like a deer in the headlights, or they are steeped in denial and refuse to recognize what could happen. They pretend everything is all right and that nothing can go wrong. It is a rigid and ineffective way to deal with crises; Freud felt that denial was a primitive defense or coping mechanism. Denial is not the best way to cope with challenges; knowing your options is a better way. Once you're aware of your choices and what to expect, you can prepare for anything that could happen. It gives you power, choices, and control over what you can and should do next. Knowing what could be coming makes you feel ready for anything; you won't feel trapped because you have other solutions to pursue. You feel empowered and energized, and you have a sense of hope and purpose. You can face reality with confidence.

So when you have a dilemma, make a list from Best Scenario to Worst Scenario of all the possible outcomes—from the ideal to the possible, all the way down to the acceptable and the abysmal. Really "catastrophize" so you can be prepared for anything that could happen! For example, if you would like a raise and yet you're afraid to confront your boss, compile a list of all the reasons that you think you deserve a raise. Then, using the exercise below, make a list of all the things that could happen, from best to worst.

Best Scenario to Worst Scenario Exercise

If you are looking for a raise, here's what your list might look like from best to worst:

1. Not only do I get a raise, but I also get a promotion and a job title change, with the possibility of some travel. The boss apologizes for overlooking my excellence and dedication and tells me what a hardworking, loyal, and bright employee I am.

2. I get a bigger raise than I ask for because my boss sees that I deserve it and I've earned it. He apologizes for taking so long.
3. I get exactly the raise that I asked for and my boss says I've earned it.
4. My boss says that it's a possibility and that he would like to revisit this in a month.
5. My boss says that it's not a possibility right now because of the economy and the cutbacks that he has to make. He apologizes and says right now there is a freeze on hiring, promotions, and raises. He asks for my understanding, thanks me for my loyalty and hard work, and tells me he'll revisit this at a later date.
6. My boss refuses to give me a raise and won't give me any reason for it.
7. My boss refuses to give me a raise and says I don't deserve one at all at this time. He asks me to leave his office.
8. My boss admonishes me for my arrogance and tells me that I certainly do not deserve a raise and asks me to leave his office.
9. My boss is angry that I had the nerve to ask him for a raise. Then he threatens to fire me if I ever have the hubris to ask such a question again. He asks me to leave his office.
10. My boss is angry I asked him for a raise and calls me arrogant, insensitive, and out of touch with the economic times. He gives me a thirty-day notice to leave my position and train my assistant to take over my job. He says I can have thirty more days of insurance and then I can choose COBRA or find my own coverage.
11. My boss is furious that I asked him for a raise, fires me on the spot, gives me two weeks of severance pay, and tells me to clean out my desk and leave.
12. My boss is so angry I asked him for a raise that he fires me right there in his office, makes a call to HR, and when I get back to my desk, security and HR are standing there with a box, telling me to clean out my desk. Other employees witness this, and I'm embarrassed and humiliated. HR asks me for my keys and security badges, and then security walks me past my co-workers and escorts me out the door.

There may be other outcomes or combinations of the above scenarios, but you get the picture. These are the types of possibilities that can result from any action that you may take, so it's greatly beneficial to visualize what can happen when you take a risk. When you make your list, allow for the possibility that even better or worse things could also happen.

Making this list is *not* an attempt to force a self-fulfilling prophecy. Rather, this is an exercise that allows you to brainstorm everything that *might* occur so you can prepare yourself for any of the outcomes, whether negative or positive. After that you must take each possible result—both positive and negative—and contemplate the effects if each one really were to happen. Are you psychologically and financially prepared for each option? This exercise will help you find out so that you can properly assess the risk.

A Look at Potential Negative Outcomes

Let's take a look at the negative outcomes that could result after you ask for a raise:

1. If you don't get the raise, can you still live on what you're making? If you can't live on what you're making, could and should you realistically take a second job?
2. If you're fired, do you have enough money in the bank to ensure that your bills will be paid and that you can pay for COBRA's increased health insurance costs? How many months can you live without going broke or having unpaid bills affect your credit rating?
3. Do you have a spouse who can carry the financial burden for a while? If so, for how long? If the spouse needs to find a job or work outside the home, can he or she do that now, without training or classes?
4. Do you have parents, relatives, or friends who can lend you money to get through? If so, how much and for how long? Are you ready to sign a contract with them for repayment?
5. Is your résumé up-to-date? Are you ready to begin interviewing? Do you need to go to a résumé service to assist in this, or do you have friends who can do it for you for free?

6. What companies have openings and seem interesting to work at? What word-of-mouth openings do your friends and colleagues know about? Do you have an "in" or any connections at any companies to get hired?
7. Should you switch professions? Is it time to start your own business? What is it that you've always wanted to do?
8. Do you have friends who want to start a business together? Do you need funding? If so, can you get it from a bank, backers, investors, or other partners? Do you have a business plan? What do you need to launch this enterprise?
9. Do you have to move? If so, will you have to sell your home/condo or rent it out? What is the job market like? Will you lose or gain money on the sale?
10. Psychologically, are you up to all of this? Do you need some emotional support, counseling, psychotherapy, marriage/couples counseling with your spouse to get through this transition? Find a counselor who has experience in this area and schedule some sessions.

A Look at Potential Positive Outcomes

Now if you get the raise or promotion, let's take the positives and also prepare for some challenges:

1. Will you be working with anyone you have heard is notoriously difficult? How do you want to prepare for that? Will the promotion be worth the difficulties or negativities of working with this negative person?
2. Should you take some management courses? Will the company train you for your new position? Will the company pay for any continuing education classes you might need?
3. Are you truly ready for the promotion? Do you feel nervous, scared, and possibly not up to the challenge? Do you need to read some books and get some counseling to get through this transition?
4. Can you now get that larger apartment you've been dreaming of, or can you afford to buy a home or condo with the increased income?

5. Should you wait on the move to see if the new job is a good fit before making any changes or spending any money?
6. Do you need some new clothes for this advanced position? Is it in your budget?
7. Do you have a tendency to spend more when you have more money coming in? If so, is that something you need to monitor or eliminate in difficult economic times? Would a bookkeeper or an accountant help to keep you in check from going overboard?
8. Is there a possibility it won't work out and you could get demoted or transferred? If so, to where and doing what?
9. If it doesn't work out, could you get fired? What are your options then? If it all does work out, is there another chance for promotion? Will you be ready for that?
10. Are you taking courses for an advanced degree to prepare for the next step up the ladder—your M.B.A., Ph.D., or other credentials?

Doing the best scenario to worst scenario exercise empowers you. It gives you the confidence of being prepared for anything that could happen—both positive and negative. After analyzing the list of possibilities, do you conclude that the negative risks are greater than you'd like to gamble on right now? If so, and if the present financial climate is an especially tight economy and you don't feel comfortable taking a chance on asking for a raise, then don't do it. Perhaps you can wait until the economy improves to ask for it. Or is this an opportunity that could send your entire career on a better path?

After you've exhausted all the foreseeable possibilities and feel prepared, then it's time to start your visualization on the most positive outcome. Before you get out of bed each morning, before you fall asleep, during your lunch hour—basically whenever you have a moment—force yourself to see that ideal outcome in your mind's eye. Visualizing the outcome you want to happen truly can help to make it happen. Positive thoughts go a long way toward creating positive realities.

CHAPTER 19

Keep Your Expectations Reasonable and Your Hopes High

One reason people get angry is that their expectations are out of line with reality. In the previous exercise, "Best Scenario to Worst Scenario," you outlined all of what could happen if you decided to take a risk at work. Doing so gives you the power to prepare for any one of those results. The second part of this preparation is to make sure that you have realistic expectations. Sometimes, if you have very high expectations, then the slightest bit of disappointment can wreck your day. You must build in a flexible margin of acceptability. If you always expect 100 percent positive results from everything you do, you might find yourself feeling disappointed even when you get 99 percent of what you wanted! Feeling this way can sap your energy, make you depressed, and waste your precious time. And it is ridiculous when you look at the fact that you achieved 99 percent of your goal, which is just about perfect!

Let's make a distinction here between a negative self-fulfilling prophecy and being prepared for the worst. If you constantly think you will be given less than you deserve, feel that life has treated you unkindly, and have negative or minimal expectations from the world, then most likely you will receive just what you've come to expect. That line of thinking is what makes a negative self-fulfilling prophecy come to fruition. When you expect the worst from the world, life has a way of making manifest what your negative thoughts and beliefs have created. This outcome then reinforces your feeling that life is unfair—even though you've contributed to the negative outcome yourself! When you get the negative outcome you expected, it "proves" that you are a worthless, undeserving loser. Thinking this way perpetuates a vicious circle.

On the other hand, being prepared for a disappointment and knowing what options you have in case it actually happens is very different. You're prepared but not dwelling on the negative thoughts or giving them power. You can instead opt to take action immediately to correct the situation. So, if and when these potential outcomes present themselves, you will have the knowledge, power, and choice to handle and dispel them. That is the earmark of a smart person who is prepared psychologically and reinforces what a previous chapter stated: "Forewarned is forearmed."

Reading books on positive thinking, from Norman Vincent Peale, Wayne Dyer, Claude Bristol, Deepak Chopra, and many others can show you the power of your thoughts and your mind to create the reality that you would like. There will always be the polarity and consequences for choices; however, you can create the job, the life, and work environment that you envision and desire.

CHAPTER 20

Assertive Techniques That Give You Power

Here are the steps of assertiveness when you are taking the risk of confronting another person in the workplace, be it a co-worker or a supervisor:

1. **State the problem.** Use the Sandwich Technique. Start with a positive compliment about the person, then go directly into the problem, giving feedback clearly and with specific examples, and end on a positive note.
2. **State your feelings.** Say how the person's behavior makes you feel and why. Be specific.
3. **Offer solutions.** Give the person you are confronting various options for rectifying his or her behavior and let the person know how much better your working arrangement will be when his or her behavior changes.
4. **Listen to response and feedback.** Be quiet and listen to the person's response and feedback to what you just said. Take notes so you can respond to everything he or she said.
5. **Dialogue.** Have an honest discussion, listen without interrupting the other person, and comment on each thing he or she says. Be prepared to hear comments on each thing you have said and respond accordingly.

6. **Resolution.** Decide what the action plan will be and agree on it, perhaps in writing.
7. **Follow up.** Send a letter and/or e-mail summarizing what the resolution was and, if the situation calls for it, copy it to whomever might also be affected—bosses, other co-workers, and so forth.
8. **Give an ultimatum, if necessary.** If the person you are confronting refuses to change, or if you've given him or her plenty of time to alter the behavior but he or she has not done so, then it may be necessary to lay down an ultimatum. State what you intend to do if compliance isn't achieved and be specific. If you're going to report the behavior to a supervisor or to HR, let the person know who you will be reporting it to and when you plan on doing so.

Example of Using the Steps of Assertiveness

Let's look at an abbreviated example of an employee named Bob and his co-worker Jack. Bob has a problem that he needs to confront Jack about. Bob started out using the Sandwich and then followed the standard steps of assertiveness. Presented here are two separate examples—one with a more positive discussion and outcome, and one with a more negative outcome—to compare. See the advantages of the positive discussion and you can use that as your model.

State the Problem(s)

Bob: *Jack, you've been a valued co-worker here for five years. We've noticed your work isn't coming in on time and I'm wondering what's wrong. Why is it happening and is there anything I or the company can do to help you meet your deadlines?*

POSITIVE RESPONSE

Jack: *I'm sorry. I apologize.*

NEGATIVE RESPONSE

Jack: *Get off my back. What business is it of yours?*

State Your Feelings

Bob: *When your work isn't completed on time, it slows down the whole department because we all depend on your reports. I'm responsible for you and I need to know what's wrong. When you don't tell me what's happening, I feel cut off and that makes me upset. Also I'm getting pressure from my boss to see to it that every member of the team delivers his or her work on time.*

POSITIVE RESPONSE

Jack: *We're all under pressure and I'm sorry I made you feel that way.*

NEGATIVE RESPONSE

Jack: *Don't give me your guilt trip—I'm working as hard as I can.*

Offer Solutions

Bob: *What can I do to help you get the reports in on time? Do you need an administrative assistant for a few days? Do you need to partner up with someone to share the workload? Are there any problems at work I can take care of?*

POSITIVE RESPONSE

Jack: *Yes, I'd like an assistant to help me get caught up. That would really help.*

NEGATIVE RESPONSE

Jack: *I don't need any help, least of all from you. Get off my back.*

Listen to Feedback

POSITIVE FEEDBACK

Jack: *You've been patient and I apologize for not telling you sooner. I thought I could catch up and I don't want to make the department late for deadlines. I'm sorry.*

NEGATIVE FEEDBACK

Jack: *I don't appreciate being singled out like this. Shouldn't you be on somebody else's case right now? It's ridiculous that you think I'm the one dragging this team down.*

Dialogue

Bob: *I understand that you thought you could get everything done without coming to me, and now you see that you couldn't. I know how hard you're working and what pressure you must feel. Let's see how we can remedy this.*

POSITIVE RESPONSE

Jack: *I should have come to you before. I appreciate your willingness to help me.*

NEGATIVE RESPONSE

Jack: *You never listen to me so why would I have come to you for help before?*
Bob: *It's OK, I understand. I'm listening now and I'm willing to help.*

Resolution

Bob: *So, Jack, do we have an agreement that you'll get your reports in on time in the future and ask for help if you need it?*

POSITIVE RESPONSE

Jack: *Yes. I'll come in early if I need to and get caught up. Thanks for understanding. If you need anything else, let me know.*

NEGATIVE RESPONSE

Jack: *This is ludicrous! I'm not agreeing to anything.*

Follow Up

A wise co-worker always summarizes meetings in a hand-delivered memo or an e-mail with the recommendations and agreed-upon plan, and if the situation calls for it, copies to HR and a supervisor. Include a sentence at the end such as, "If you have any questions about or additions to this memo, please respond in writing." Following up allows the co-worker recourse to respond and ensures that you're covered, which is crucial in any company, whether you are the co-worker, boss, or owner. People can say, "I never said that," or "I didn't agree to that," but if you put it in writing, then you're covered and they can defend themselves and respond.

Give Ultimatum(s)

Bob: *If you can't get the reports in on time, let me know. If your work continues to be late, please know that you are jeopardizing your position at the company and you may be demoted or fired, and I would not like to see that happen.*

POSITIVE RESPONSE

Jack: *I didn't realize I was in that much trouble here. I totally understand, and thanks for telling me.*

NEGATIVE RESPONSE

Jack: *Don't make threats that you can't back up—you don't have the power to fire me.*

Bob should send an e-mail to Jack, summarizing the above conversation and the agreements made. He should also copy it to those above him in the company as proof of him taking care of the situation and Jack's compliance or refusal to remedy the late reports.

Being Assertive with Your Boss

Communicating with a co-worker is different from communicating with your boss, yet there are similarities. With both a co-worker and a boss, you want to be tactful, diplomatic, clear, and firm. And it's best for it to be done away from others—co-workers, other executives or staff—perhaps at lunch or before or after work. If the situation is so dire that getting out of the office isn't possible, use an empty conference room, office, or lunchroom, always checking to make sure that no one is within earshot. If one of you has a private office or there's one available, use it and shut the door.

With a boss, you are coming in as an employee, not as a peer. Any negative feedback given to a boss could be interpreted by some as insubordination and grounds to fire you, and nobody wants to lose a job unnecessarily. However, if you can no longer tolerate a boss's behavior, then you must take action. Be as diplomatic as you possibly can. Be aware that your boss is a human being like anyone else and no one likes to lose face or be humiliated. Don't play the part of a scolding parent; rather, go to your boss from a place of respect.

Some people don't want to risk direct confrontation with a boss, and so they go directly to HR and file a complaint. That is always an option. Remember, however, that your HR representative may be on the side of the boss and the administration. He or she may do whatever necessary to squash dissent. If so, you have other options, discussed in future chapters, such as going to your boss's boss, the union, trade association or professional organization, the ACLU, the NAACP, the Women's Defense Fund of the National Organization for Women, or government agencies like EEOC; getting an attorney and filing a lawsuit; and going to the media. If the work environment is dangerous, you can report it to OSHA or seek out a news reporter who handles such stories.

Sometimes having the head of HR act as a facilitator in your conflict can be quite beneficial, though. You would want to do this if your boss has given any indication that he or she would be unreasonable in a private discussion. Having the conversation in front of the HR representative puts everything out in the open right away. If the situation is extremely tense, you may even want to ask an attorney to come with you or at least be there on a conference call.

If you decide to confront your boss directly, which can be the preferred first step, then start off the conversation as you would with a co-worker—on a positive note, stating what you like about your job, the company, and working for him or her. Then let your boss know what he or she has been doing that has made you uncomfortable, unhappy, or frustrated, and the effect it has had on you. Follow the same pattern of assertiveness techniques listed above. Be careful about stating the ultimatum, unless you are sure you can state one and have it received positively and enforce it yourself.

Handling a Toxic Boss Yourself

Here are some general guidelines for handling a toxic boss by yourself:

1. Know what your issues are. Make a list of exactly what you want to say and keep the notes with you when you have the meeting. Nervousness and anxiety make us forget what we want to say and the notes can help us remember.

2. In addition to your notes, you may want to write and send a letter or e-mail first, outlining your issues, your feelings, and your proposed solutions. This may be a way of showing your boss that you mean business, you have given this a great deal of thought, and you intend to reach a beneficial solution to both you and the company. If you *cc* it at the bottom to your attorney, then it has even more weight. Companies and bosses do not like lawsuits.
3. Rehearse the conversation in front of a mirror or with a friend. Ask your friend for feedback. Try audio- or videotaping yourself so you can hear and see how you sound and what you look like. Critique your own performance. Do it again and again until you feel comfortable.
4. In the letter or the e-mail or when you speak to your boss in person, ask when a good time would be to get together to discuss your issues.
5. Establish some ground rules at the start of the meeting—no interruptions, turn off cell phones and office phones, let each person finish what he or she has to say and then respond; keep everything confidential.
6. State that your intention is to have a win/win outcome, that you are open to hearing what your boss has to say, and that you want to resolve this amiably.
7. Be neatly dressed, act professionally, stand up straight with shoulders back, and use a pleasant tone of voice, not in a bullying stance or tone or a whining, victim stance or tone.
8. Use solid eye contact—do not look off at the ceiling or the floor. Say what you mean and mean what you say.
9. Know what you have control over and what you don't. Don't give ultimatums if you can't back them up with action. Be prepared to be fired, as you have learned in Chapter 18.
10. Use the Sandwich Technique. Start out positively and give compliments, state what negative issues need to be addressed, and end up positively with a statement that you want to resolve this with a win/win result.

11. Don't attack or blame. Keep the communication as a calm description of a certain behavior that he or she does, how it affects you, and how you would like it to be.
12. Use "I" statements—"I feel this way when you do that," or "When you say or do that, it makes me feel this way." Always own your reactions and perceptions.
13. If the boss says, "Other people don't feel that way . . ." simply keep on track by saying something along the lines of "But it's how *I feel* and I have a right to tell you and get it resolved." Other people may not have the same feelings or reactions as you; you have the right to discuss how your boss's behavior makes you feel, and you have a right to ask him or her to change.
14. Give clear, simple solutions—"I'd prefer it if you would do this"—and be very specific on how and in what ways you would like the behavior to change.
15. Sometimes meeting and talking over lunch or at a restaurant helps to lessen the impact, since food can absorb tension, plus having others around in a restaurant can ensure a calmer exchange without raised voices, outbursts, or the potential of violence.
16. After you finish, give the boss a chance to respond. *Listen* to what he or she has to say without interrupting and use active listening—paraphrase what you hear him or her saying to you.
17. If the boss starts to attack you, say that you'd like to hear any complaints he or she may have about you, and that those need to wait until you're finished. Stay on the original topic at hand; don't be misled or distracted from what you're there to discuss. Guard against "the Boomerang" that others may use.
18. Keep a copy of the letter or e-mail that you wrote (in step 2 above) with you and hand the letter to the toxic boss after the encounter. If you already had sent a copy, give him or her another copy as a reminder that you mean business. This can be the first document that you use as proof of you warning him or her about the dysfunctional behavior.

19. If you run out of time, reschedule the next appointment so you can resolve your issues. Thank the boss for giving you the opportunity to discuss this. If it's not resolved, offer other options: to reschedule another appointment, perhaps even later the same day, go to a mediator, go to HR, or keep talking about it between the two of you until it's resolved.
20. Follow up with an e-mail directly to your boss. And make sure you *cc* it at the bottom to your attorney, his boss, HR, and/or other involved parties. If this is an initial attempt to resolve it without involving them, then don't. But it's better to cover yourself from the start with an attorney, HR, and your boss's boss. Review and recap your perceptions of the discussion. You need to do this in case of any legal repercussions in the future. Keep these copies in a safe, locked place, such as a safe-deposit box at the bank.

With all these techniques, examples, and suggestions, I hope you've learned that you can confront obnoxious co-workers and difficult bosses with diplomacy, patience, and self-assurance. You may be pleasantly surprised with what you can change. You probably have more power than you think you do!

PART III

STAFF INFECTIONS

How to Recognize and Handle Toxic People

CHAPTER 21

How to Deal with Toxic Co-Workers

S.E.S.S.I.O.N.: The Situation, Explanation, and Solution System in Overcoming Nuisances

After reading the previous chapters, you have had a general and condensed course in powerful communication techniques that will help you resolve issues. Now it's time to bring them all together and put them into action for your specific needs. In this section of the book, I describe the many different types of toxic co-workers and bosses you may have to confront to make your work situation more agreeable, and exactly how to go about doing so. An acronym I like to use for these confrontations is S.E.S.S.I.O.N.: The Situation, Explanation, and Solution System in Overcoming Nuisances! Each specific type of toxic personality is discussed in the following chapters in three categories:

1. First, the *Situation* with each toxic personality is briefly described. These are my estimations of what you are probably experiencing with each toxic person, what they may say and do that drive you crazy, and how you probably feel.

2. Next is the *Explanation*, detailing *why* these toxic people usually do what they do. I attempt to briefly theorize and describe what psychological factors would cause the behavior. By doing this, I hope you develop a compassionate understanding of the possible childhood influences that have gone into making people act the way they do. Please notice how the minds, hearts, and motivations of these toxic people are functioning. I'm not condoning their behavior or making excuses for it. I'm simply positing what might be the cause of it and asking you to understand it when you deal directly with the person. You have your own issues, motivations, and quirks as we all do, so be mindful of the adage and song lyrics, "Walk a mile in my shoes before you criticize and accuse."
3. Finally, I offer a proposed *Solution* with a specific and direct way to deal with each person of this type. The solution is presented in the form of a practice monologue, which, of course, you can adapt, change, and tailor to your specific needs and circumstances. It may help you to write out what you want to say and memorize the lines, just as an actor does for a play. You must feel comfortable and familiar with the words, be able to think on your feet, and feel relaxed enough to improvise if the person throws a verbal curve ball at you.

Remember, you will most likely be met with denial, resistance, refutation, and accusations of similar or offending behavior that you do because most people don't want to admit their flaws, are resistant to change, and are angry when made to look at their behavior. If you're prepared for these reactions, then you will be able to proceed confidently, addressing the toxic behaviors of your co-workers, which you hope they can and will change in virtually no time.

To help you understand yourself better, I recommend that you also look at why these toxic people with their negative behaviors bug you so much. Why are you letting them get to you? Do they remind you of what you don't like in yourself? Are they thorns in your side because of the way your own mother, father, relatives, siblings, or teachers behaved toward you as a child? If so, then I strongly recommend that you think about these factors *before* you confront them.

Perhaps there is a lesson here for you to learn. People are put in our path for many reasons, one of which is so we can learn from them. So be your own shrink and do some work on yourself first. You will have more insight and compassion and you will be better prepared when you do confront them.

Types of Toxic Co-Workers

As Mark Twain said, "Find a job you love, and you'll never work a day in your life." That is certainly true, and you may love your job, but you also have to deal with toxic and crazy people in the workplace. In this part, disruptive co-workers are grouped according to the following twelve major categories as to how they are distracting, disgusting, disruptive, or dangerous. Each group is then handled in its own chapter.

The Socially Clueless

The Rude One
The Insensitive One
The Busybody/The Gossip
The Loud One
The Braggart
The Bossy One
The Interrupter
The Hermit

The Work Interferers

The Disgusting One
The Noise Maker
The Talker
The Deal Maker
The Erratic One
The Incompetent
The Chronically Late One
The Big-Picture Person
The Detail Person
The Procrastinator
The Narcissist
The Drama Queen

The Uncommitted

The Rock Star/The Actor
The Day-Job Worker
The Sloth
The Avoider

The Angry Ones

The Fighter
The Verbal Attacker
The Threatener
The Provoker

The Politically Incorrect

The Hater
The Sexist
The Ageist

The Homophobe
The Wasteful One
The Non-PC Joke Teller

The Victims

The Fearful One
The Delicate Flower
The Victim
The Martyr
The Whiner
The Crybaby
The Chaos Creator
The Money Borrower

The Rescuers

The Arranger
The Problem Solver
The Mother Hen

The Saboteurs

The Passive-Aggressive
The Silent Treatment
The Sugarcoater
The Smiling Cobra
The Thief
The Idea and Credit Stealer
The Naysayer
The Envious One
The Practical Joker

The Politicians

The Political Soap Boxer
The Office Politician
The Brownnoser
The Ladder Climber
The Boss's Relative

The Sexually Suggestive

The Seducer/The Seductress
The Flatterer
The Flirt
The Sexual Harasser
The Office Couple
The Office Affair
The Jealous One/The Stalker
The Mistress
The Boy Toy

The Obsessives

The Missionary
The Food Faddist
The Paranoid
The Perfectionist
The Control Freak
The Critic

The Addicts

The Alcoholic/The Drug Addict/The Addictive Personality
The Enabler/The Codependent
The Chronic Shopper
The Gambler
The Pornographer

CHAPTER 22

The Socially Clueless

The Rude One

The Insensitive One

The Busybody/The Gossip

The Loud One

The Braggart

The Bossy One

The Interrupter

The Hermit

As a category, the socially clueless—those co-workers with poor social skills—can be rude, impolite, insensitive, tactless, or any combination of those traits. They can be oblivious to normal social cues and rules, or they can and will deliberately defy social conventions to get what they want. They may be nosy, intrusive, and eager to pry into someone's life, interested in finding out negative personal information about someone else or willing to invent it and spread false rumors. They behave this way for any number of reasons: to use the information against someone else, discredit someone, or just to have something "interesting" to talk about. They may seem ditzy or clueless, and many in this group are, or they can be vicious, conniving, and vindictive. Perhaps they had parents who didn't have advanced social skills themselves and never taught their children how to be observant and sensitive to the feelings of others, to read body language, to pick up on social cues, and to be tactful, gracious, and diplomatic. These people usually don't have a high level of empathy and can be boorish and oafish as well as jealous, envious, and sometimes just evil.

To deal effectively with this type of person, you must do your research and have proof of the misdeeds, such as e-mails, documents, or witnesses who will go to bat for you. You need to collect evidence so that you can confront the person with facts. You should be polite and direct, and let the person know that you are aware of what he or she has done. Do not be bought off by denials, apologies, explanations, or "Yes, but . . ." answers because all of that is usually an act and the person will just go on to do it again.

The Rude One

Situation

Rudy the Rude is incredibly insensitive. He says and does obnoxious things with seemingly no understanding of how his behavior may be offensive or hurt someone's feelings. Rudy can be an equal opportunity offender—any race, class, ethnic group, gender, or sexual preference can be and usually is a target. Rudy may be clueless, but he may deliberately be doing it to bait you into a fight. He may have the emotional hide of a rhino and thinks you do, too.

Explanation

Rudy may have been brought up by people who were totally without social graces, so he never had the role model of someone who cared how other people felt. His parents likely demonstrated their ill manners and lack of breeding regularly, with the result that your co-worker now behaves toxically because he doesn't know any other way.

Rudy behaves like a Mack truck that just barrels through life, not knowing or caring whom he offends, who's in his way, or whom he hurts. People like Rudy may fully intend to feel as though they're in control just to put people off their game. They like rattling people's cages and being the smart aleck in the class. They feel they get the psychological upper hand this way.

Solution

It will take tact, strength, and assertiveness to educate people like Rudy to become more sensitive. They have to know there will be consequences for their repeated infractions or they won't change. The first time Rudy crosses the line, pull him aside and say:

Rudy, what you just said hurt my feelings and it was terribly rude. I've heard you say things like that before to other people, and they've had the same reaction, whether or not they've said anything to you. In the future, please say nothing at all. If you have a question for me, you can ask me individually, away from others. I would recommend that you read some books on etiquette, politeness, and communication. You're not winning friends around the office with this kind of behavior. Are you aware of this? If it doesn't change, I may have to go to HR to file a complaint. I hope you will be more aware of this in the future so we can have a cooperative working environment. I know you're a smart, capable person and I'd like for us to get along and for you to use better manners.

Hopefully, Rudy will comply after he's confronted, and if so, you should give him positive reinforcement for doing so. If Rudy doesn't comply, you can warn him again, and this time, give him an ultimatum: "Rudy, you're still saying rude and inappropriate things and it needs to stop or I'm going to have to report you to our boss and to HR." And if he doesn't comply, then report him. You may get other input and witnesses from your co-workers, and if you don't, do it yourself.

The Insensitive One

Situation

Inez the Insensitive is like Rudy in many ways but she may be more clueless than Rudy, who can be deliberately mean-spirited, cruel, and vicious. Inez will hurt your feelings because she is like a bull in a china shop, just barging in without any awareness of the sensitive situation she is in.

Explanation

Inez the Insensitive is oblivious to others' feelings. She seems to be missing the "sensitivity chip" that can be found in most people. Inez doesn't read body language, take hints, or understand how delicate some people's feelings can be—or if she does, she simply doesn't care. Make a list of her transgressions and confront her with them; people like Inez have to have "proof" or they still won't get it. You have to hold a mirror up to Inez for her to understand what she is doing to you and everyone else. Otherwise she will remain oblivious to the effects of her insensitivity.

Solution

Inez, I like the work you do here in the office. I've noticed, though, that you have sometimes hurt people's feelings with your insensitive handling of situations. I'd like to give you a few examples so that you know exactly what I'm talking about. [Here you would enumerate the reasons why Inez's insensitivity has become a problem. If you mention times where she has been insensitive toward other people, then be sure to let her know that these are instances that you observed, unless the person who was directly affected approached you and asked for you to confront Inez on his or her behalf.] Inez, when you don't have anything nice to say, please don't say anything at all. You will save yourself the embarrassment, anger, and ill will that you are creating against you. I hope you'll heed my words, Inez. I know you're a hard worker and we all need to get along with each other here, and I hope we can.

The Busybody/The Gossip

Situation

Gracie the Gossip is nosy, snoopy, and gossipy. She likes to spread rumors, innuendoes, and stories. She likes to know everything she can about other people's business for many different reasons. That means she will snoop and eavesdrop on her co-workers and then tell tales about what she's heard. Gracie asks personal questions that are really none of her business—about your income, sexual relationships, marriage, children, age, weight, and every other issue. Just when you think Gracie can't get any more intrusive, she comes up with another unsettling question. You stand there, shocked at her lack of tact and social skills. You really don't know what to say. Many times you are shocked at her intrusiveness, and you feel as though you have to do something to stop her. The good news is that you can.

Explanation

Gracie probably had parents or relatives who learned to use information as leverage and emotional blackmail—whether at home, in their personal lives, or at work—to get the upper hand. Perhaps her father or mother was an attorney or a private investigator. She likes to gain and gather information that she may use against you in the future. The depth of her personal questions simply knows no bounds. Perhaps during her childhood Gracie was ignored or shunned by the "in" crowd. The way she learned to get back at them was through gathering information, finding out their secrets, and then spreading rumors and gossip. This may be her unconscious revenge on the rest of the world for the rejection she experienced in school. Gracie is probably not a happy person. Behavior like hers is in keeping with someone who is enormously insecure and really lonely inside. People like Gracie don't trust others, and they don't make good friends because their confidentiality can't be trusted. They usually don't want to feel vulnerable so they become convinced that they are perfect and that *you* are the one with the problems. When it comes to dealing with Gracie, you must be able to set the boundaries and, in clear terms, inform her that it's simply none of her business.

Solution

Gracie, I respect how hard you work and I would like to maintain a cooperative working relationship with you. I have discovered that you have been saying unflattering things about me around the office, and they simply are not true. These rumors have damaged my reputation and hurt my feelings, and I'm angry about it. I resent you gossiping about me and spreading false rumors like this. I ask that you apologize and send an e-mail to people in the office, stating that you were wrong and that you're sorry. I'd like to continue to work with you in this office. If you don't do this, though, you'll force me to go to HR to handle this. Are you willing to send an e-mail and apologize? I hope so because I truly want for us to get along together.

If Gracie agrees, follow up to make sure everyone gets a copy of her e-mail. Put the incident behind you and continue your working relationship with Gracie. Keep a close eye on her, though, because usually these types either continue to gossip or they find someone else to gossip about. You trust someone like Gracie with personal information at your own peril. She can't be trusted.

If Gracie refuses to apologize and write the e-mail, then you have to make good on your ultimatum and go to HR to file a formal complaint. The HR representative can also have her in for a talk, ask her about it, and even have you in to confront her directly in HR's presence. Hopefully, your HR director will either discipline Gracie or at the very least ensure that she sends an e-mail to the co-workers she spread rumors about you to, recanting those rumors.

The Loud One

Situation

Loudon the Loud One may not realize it, but his voice is very loud. He shouts when he could speak normally and he always seems to be on the phone. You don't want to bring him to client lunches because you know he's probably going to blow out the room with his volume and offend your clients. He may lose friendships and have contracts cancelled because of his irritating behavior, obnoxious personality, and loud voice.

Explanation

Loudon may have a partial hearing loss and have no idea how loud he is. Perhaps he previously had a job in a noisy area—such as a large factory, warehouse, or power plant—where he had to yell to be heard, and when he came home, he forgot to switch gears to his "inside voice," as the kindergarten teacher would say. On the other hand, Loudon could be speaking loudly deliberately to intimidate people. Or he may be doing this as a habit from childhood, and you have to remind him to speak more softly. He may have had deaf or hearing-impaired parents and had to speak loudly every day to be heard by them. You may or may not want to ask him leading questions to bring these more personal issues up when you speak with him privately, away from co-workers. A nonverbal cue, like a downward glance or a subtle finger to your lips, may be enough to help him recognize when to lower his voice.

Solution

Loudon, I like working with you and hope to continue. I have to tell you, though, that your loud voice can be rather off-putting. You may not even realize it, but you're practically yelling when you speak and we all can hear you perfectly well. We hope that you will be a bit quieter so the workplace is more tranquil. I'd like to have a nonverbal cue with you, like when I give a downward glance or put my finger to my lips, to remind you to lower your voice. Thanks for listening and taking this suggestion. I appreciate it!

The Braggart

Situation

Brad the Braggart is loud and obnoxious, talks too much, and interferes with everyone's concentration. He may also spend too much time on personal phone calls and social e-mails. Brad is constantly telling you and anyone else who will listen about his latest sexual conquest, how much money he made in a stock trade, how he just bought a new BMW—basically, anything that seems as though it would get another person full of envy. You're not getting your work done because of Brad's constant stories, and the bragging is really getting under your skin.

Explanation

Brad is probably a self-centered and insecure narcissist who has to be the center of attention. People like him tend to be blind to other people's needs and rights, and they have a huge sense of entitlement. You must make him aware of the realities of the workplace—that people have jobs to do and his bragging and interruptions are preventing them from getting everything done. Underneath, Brad has a low self-esteem or else he wouldn't feel the need to boast so much. When you confront Brad privately away from co-workers—and if his boasting has become a problem then you absolutely must—be careful that you don't step on his ego because some "Brads" can get vicious, vengeful, and vindictive. Be as pleasant and firm as you can be. Set limits and let him know you'll go to your boss or HR if his behavior doesn't change.

Solution

Brad, we appreciate your sense of humor and larger-than-life personality. You certainly seem to live an interesting life, and it's fun to hear about it sometimes. I've also noticed that you're disturbing your co-workers and me when you brag about what's going on in your life, and it needs to stop. I'm sure you're proud of your possessions, travels, and accomplishments, and we wish you the best with all of that. Perhaps you can share that with me or our other co-workers after work. We have jobs to do here, though, and we need to concentrate on getting them done. I'm sure you understand, and I hope you will take that to heart and change your interactions. Thanks for listening and understanding.

The Bossy One

Situation

Bonnie the Bossy One knows what's best for you and tells you so. Sometimes she's more like a negative mother hen—cluck, cluck, clucking away—voicing her disapproval with her tsk-tsks, telling you exactly what to do and how to do it. She feels morally superior and she can be incredibly judgmental, telling you that you're wrong and letting everyone around you hear it, too. She believes that her opinions, perception, and instructions are always correct. The bossiness can turn into an oppressive dictatorship so you need to nip this in the bud or it will only get worse.

Explanation

Bonnie has to be right. It's in her bone marrow. If she's not right, it affects her self-image, which is based on her being holier than thou. She probably had a very judgmental mother or father and learned to always do the "right" thing and be correct in all her answers at school and at home. She may be deeply religious, although without understanding the most important messages of religion—love, compassion, mercy, and understanding. She is a control freak, and it's her way or the highway. Whether Bonnie is a female or a male, she or he may have grown up in a military family, served in the military herself or himself, and may think that the company needs to be run like a regiment. She or he may be used to barking orders and having them obeyed without question. Bonnie's bossiness may also come out sugarcoated or with passive-aggressive remarks. No matter which way, though, you are going to hear it from her. Bonnie is not your boss or your life coach, she's your co-worker; however, she simply won't accept that reality. By confronting her, you are helping her accept that fact. If it doesn't improve, you will need to go to HR or your boss.

Solution

Bonnie, you have some really great ideas and I do, too, and so do our other co-workers. Everyone would like to be heard and we'd all like to contribute and not be told what to do or that our opinions and choices are wrong, which is what you often say when people don't agree with you. If you have feedback about how to make something better, then by all means, share what you think. However, please do so in a positive way without putting other people and their ideas down. You can say why you believe your ideas will work, just please back them up with facts. When you're refuting what someone else has said, it's difficult to take you at your word without any proof. When you don't agree, you can say why you don't agree when someone asks for your opinion. Just be open and up-front about what you don't agree with, OK? Thanks!

The Interrupter

Situation

Ian the Interrupter constantly cuts you off in midsentence and never lets you finish your thought. It's annoying, frustrating, and sometimes he's just plain wrong—you don't need anyone finishing your sentences for you. If he'd just shut up and listen, he wouldn't have so many questions and you wouldn't have to repeat yourself and get so frustrated. Perhaps Ian thinks what you have to say is stupid, doesn't want to hear it, and has no patience whatsoever.

Explanation

Perhaps when Ian was a child, he never got to express his opinion so he felt the need to interrupt others at an early age. He may discount others' opinions, and he may have ADD or ADHD, which makes it hard for him to concentrate on what you're saying. He may be trying to prove to you how smart or intuitive he is by "reading your thoughts" or finishing your sentences for you. It's also Ian's way to "cut you off at the pass" for information he doesn't want to hear. He doesn't want to be confronted, so he interrupts you. Getting interrupted frequently can make a person feel devalued and less confident in his or her opinions. If someone is making you feel this way at work, you have no choice but to say something.

Solution

Ian, I would like to maintain a cooperative working relationship with you. It seems every time I'm talking to you, you interrupt me. If you'd just listen and let me finish what I want to say, I wouldn't feel so frustrated, you would hear everything I need to tell you, and you wouldn't have to ask me questions. I've noticed that you do this to others, not just me. Please be more aware of when other people are having a conversation, have the patience to wait until they're finished, and then talk to me. If it's an absolute emergency, that's a different story, but we rarely have any emergencies in this department. I hope you can become aware of this and stop it so we can work cooperatively together. I'd like that!

If Ian agrees with what you're saying, you'll be fine. Put the confrontation behind you and go on with your business. However, if Ian continues to interrupt you and others, remind him each time he does it. Then warn him that you are willing to bring the matter to the attention of HR or your boss if he refuses to change his ways and do it if there's no improvement.

The Hermit

Situation

Henry the Hermit is the opposite of Alice the Arranger or Molly the Mother Hen (see Chapter 28). Henry is probably an introvert and an avoider who doesn't want to be bothered. If he could work at home, he would. He eats lunch at his desk or goes outside to avoid having to deal with people, and he doesn't socialize in or out of the workplace. If you're the one who is assigned to get him out of his shell, it's a difficult task. If Henry does his work on time, there's no problem, but when he starts falling down on the job, it's difficult to get him to comply because he's so reclusive and uncommunicative. Talk with him privately, never in front of others, to respect his sensitivity and confidentiality.

Explanation

If Henry is an introvert and afraid of people, he may be painfully shy. He may have been hurt in relationships, or he may have been abused as a child and is filled with memories of mental, physical, or emotional abuse and he does everything he can to avoid human contact, which was fraught with betrayal, horror, and sadness. He may be lonely or he may be perfectly satisfied with his life as it is. There are some people who have no desire to be parents, to be married, or to be in relationships—whether intimate ones or just friendships. Henry may be one of those people, so give him some space and understanding. However, if he is not doing his job, you may need help from your boss or HR to get Henry into meetings regarding his noncompliance.

Solution

Henry, I'm very respectful of your privacy and of people needing to be by themselves. I see that you like to be by yourself and you don't socialize much at all. I'm OK with that, except now your reports are missing crucial facts that you are supposed to provide, and we need you to complete your work. When I have attempted to speak to you about this, you have avoided me. You don't return my e-mails or phone calls, and we can't seem to have a conversation. When I have tried to talk to you about it, you have ignored me or walked away, and I see you doing the same thing to other co-workers. Is there something you need in order to get your work done, like an assistant or more advance notice of deadlines? I need to know so that we can resolve this situation. I feel that if we can't resolve this, I'm going to have to go to our boss or HR to resolve it. So tell me what you'd like me to do. I'd like to work cooperatively with you and get your full and completed work in on time.

CHAPTER 23

The Work Interferers

The Disgusting One

The Noise Maker

The Talker

The Deal Maker

The Erratic One

The Incompetent

The Chronically Late One

The Big-Picture Person

The Detail Person

The Procrastinator

The Narcissist

The Drama Queen

Work interferers have annoying habits, aggravating working styles, and grating personalities that interrupt your day, interfere with your getting your work started or finished, and cause you endless delays at work. The ones with disgusting personal habits can cause you to feel nauseated by the smell and sound of their repulsive hygiene. Another group has irritating habits—like singing, humming, or finger drumming—that are annoying and distracting. Occasionally these people are totally unaware they are doing it. It's usually caused by anxiety and fear. Sometimes bringing it to their attention in a gentle, compassionate way may be all they need to stop it. Other times hypnosis, acupuncture, or counseling can be helpful for them to stop.

Other work interferers talk incessantly about nothing, have unpredictable mood swings, or are always late. One type is bad enough to deal with, but you may have two or even ten in the same department who demonstrate these annoying traits. They will drag you down, involve you in their messes, and can even get you fired if you're not careful. Being aware of their habits involves realizing the reasons why these people act the way they do. Their behavior is usually based on a mixture of things: fear of success or failure, hesitation to accept responsibility, dependency on others, or a combination of these and other traits. These people must be confronted about what they do and they must stop it. It's up to you to be strong, firm, and diplomatic, and to set limits before you go to your boss or HR. If your discussion with them doesn't result in their changing, then go to your boss or HR. No one should have to put up with work interruptions.

The Disgusting One

Situation

Dirk the Disgusting makes such gross noises you feel nauseated when you hear them. He picks or loudly blows his nose, has a permeating stench of body odor or bad breath, slurps his soup, chews with his mouth full, constantly clears his throat, or is flatulent. Any one of these disgusting or annoying personal habits makes you want to reach for the gas mask and earplugs or work from home rather than sit next to Dirk. Unfortunately sometimes these unpleasant habits come in combinations.

Explanation

Usually someone with bad hygiene grew up with negligent parents who ignored these things or continued laughing when their child exhibited gross table manners long after it ceased being age-appropriate. People like Dirk may have never learned the importance of good manners. A manager might have the uncomfortable task of making Dirk cognizant of his problem and giving specific suggestions—toiletries, referrals to doctors, better clothing choices, and so forth. Usually when people like Dirk are approached, they respond in a compliant and cooperative, albeit embarrassed, fashion. A few rare exceptions will question the suggestions, in which case a manager must reiterate what is required and give a deadline for compliance. People have been fired for such transgressions, so you have a right to complain.

Solution

Dirk, you do a great deal of excellent work here. I'd like to talk to you about some habits of yours that are disturbing your co-workers. [Then be specific and name the bad habits and, depending on the offense, add something such as] Dirk, I'd like to recommend that you get some deodorant. I'm sure you understand that in close quarters, we all have to be careful of how others might be affected by our hygiene. You're a good worker and we'd like everyone here to be happy and productive. Thanks!

The Noise Maker

Situation

Sig the Singer warbles pop ditties enough to drive you nuts. She feels more at home in a karaoke bar or a church choir than in an office setting, and she probably spends her free time there, which is where the singing belongs. Whit the Whistler regrets that he couldn't have been the one who recorded the theme from "The Andy Griffith Show." Danny the Drummer wants to be Keith Moon or Ringo Starr, and he will use any surface to prove it—his desk, your desk, the watercooler, or the table. Fiona the Finger Tapper sits impatiently, watching the clock, tapping her fingers, and counting the seconds until she can leave. Just like Danny the Drummer, she too will use any surface available to take out her nervous habit in monotonous, droning rhythms that drive you crazy. Collectively, these are the office noise makers and what they do is distracting, annoying, and disturbing the work environment. It gives you a headache while you're trying to get your work done and makes you want to strangle them.

Explanation

The noise makers all have anxiety, fear, and insecurity that come out in these nervous habits. They can be totally unaware of how their nervous habits affect others, so it's your job to bring it to their attention so they can stop. If they're doing it deliberately to bug you and others, then that needs to be addressed. Sig the Singer may have a lovely voice, be a member of her church choir, and sing all the time, so she just naturally assumes that people want to hear her lilting voice. Wrong! It's distracting for most people who have work to do and need a quiet atmosphere in which to concentrate. Whit enjoys music, too, but he chooses to whistle instead of singing—and his contribution tends to be equally grating. Danny probably should be working in the music industry, where his drumming would be appreciated and valued. Fiona is just a nervous individual who needs an outlet for her anxiety, and your ears are the unlucky recipients of her jitters. Usually, the noise makers are not deliberately passive-aggressive and just need gentle reminding. If it gets intolerable, then go to your boss or HR.

Solution

Sig, you have a lovely voice and I know you love to sing, so I hope that you're a member of your church choir. It's really not appropriate for the office, though. I have work to do and I need a quiet work environment, just as others do. I would appreciate it if you would confine your singing to your shower, inside your car, or with your church choir. If you have to sing, then please do it outside during lunch or your coffee breaks. We all appreciate the work you do around here and we need a quiet office environment. If you are singing in a concert or a talent show, tell us and then we can all come to listen. I hope you will alter your behavior at the office. Thanks for understanding.

Whit, I'm sure you love music, which is why you whistle all the time. I'd be happy to listen and I'm sure it wouldn't bother me if I weren't at work. And yet, here I am at my desk with lots of research to complete, so I find your whistling distracting and it's interfering with my productivity. I'd like you to stop while you're here in the office. Please go outside and do it at lunchtime. Thanks so much for respecting the boundaries here.

Danny, I appreciate you and the work that you contribute to this company. I must say, though, that your drumming is distracting. It really needs to be reserved for activities outside of the office. Perhaps you would prefer to work at a recording studio or with a band. We've all got work to do here and I need you to be conscious of that and stop drumming. Thanks so much.

Fiona, I like your sense of humor and the quality of your work. I don't know if you're aware of your habit of finger tapping, but you seem to do it almost compulsively. I can relate because I have a lot of nervous energy, too, especially after a cup of coffee, but there has to be a quieter way to channel that energy. The finger tapping can be quite annoying and it gives people headaches. I thought I'd point it out to you so you can gain some control and stop it. I hope you can. Thanks for listening.

The Talker

Situation

Tina the Talker just yammers on and on and on, oblivious to the fact that you are working. You have assignments to complete, deadlines to meet, and Tina doesn't seem to care or even feel a need to ask if she's bothering you. Even if she saw you working, she would continue her talking. You could put in earplugs, and she still wouldn't take the hint.

Explanation

Tina loves to hear the sound of her own voice, and talking to you gives her a sense of not being alone, because she is terrified of loneliness. She probably feels bonded to you in some way, and her talking is a form of social contact for her. The sad part is that you don't even have to respond; in fact, she probably wishes you don't. She just goes on and on. If she asks you for advice and you give it, she'll gloss over it or say, "Yes, but . . . ," refuting the very advice she asked you for. It's maddening to have her as a co-worker. Solid, real friendships are two-way streets of support, empathy, caring, and mutual assistance, but if and when you ever start talking to Tina about your life, most likely she will turn a deaf ear, walk away, or tell you she has work to do. Her incessant talking is such an ingrained habit, she may not even be aware of it. You have to call it to her attention and set limits. When you tell her she must stop talking to you in order for you to get your work done, you have to stick to it. She has probably driven other co-workers crazy, and they've probably asked for transfers just to get away from her. Tina is usually a dependent personality and gets into codependent relationships. She's like a barnacle that wants to attach itself to your ship. Don't let that happen. Be strong, be firm, set limits, and mean it. If she doesn't take the hint, then a word with your boss or HR should work.

Solution

Tina, I know you have lots of things to share with me, and I'm glad you feel comfortable enough with me to be so candid. At the same time, though, I have deadlines to meet and work to do, so I really must ask you to stop talking to me unless it's very important and has something to do with work that concerns both of us. At times it feels as if you're not even talking to me, but just talking. When you ask me what I think, you don't even give me a chance to respond, as though you don't want to hear my advice. And when I talk to you about my life, you don't want to hear what I have to say. Your definition of a friendship is a one-way street—I have to listen to you, but you don't want to listen to me.

So unless you want to have an actual conversation about work, I really must ask you to let me do the work I have to do. I appreciate your honoring my request because I would like to get along with you here at work. Thanks so much, Tina!

The Deal Maker

Situation

Donald the Deal Maker always sees life as a moneyed transaction. If he does something for you, he wants something back. It's never for free or out of the kindness of his heart. He trades, barters, and manipulates. He always has an angle, like a hustler who's always trying to pull a fast one. Sometimes Donald can be suave and manipulative in an elegant, smooth, yet sneaky way. No matter what "type" Donald is, you don't trust him and you feel like you always have to watch your back around him. And you probably do!

Explanation

Donald probably had a tough life and had to work for everything he got. He may have gotten ripped off a lot by others or his parents, so he learned these hard lessons: life is tough, grab at everything you can, nothing is for free, get what you can from people, be pushy, don't be a sucker, and weakness is for saps. If he grew up in a wealthy family, he learned that money is power and that "he who has the gold makes the rules." Either way, Donald's parents probably showed him that everything was a trade, that everyone and everything had its price. You have to set limits and boundaries for Donald, refuse to trade with him, and call a process shot on him so he'll stop. He is like an addictive gambler: he loves the thrill of seeing how much he can get away with and how he can buy and sell people. Don't let him! If he doesn't stop, contact your boss or HR.

Solution

Donald, I understand that you probably have worked hard to get everything in your life, and I am tired of having every communication with you end up as some type of transaction or barter. I'm not willing to play "Let's Make a Deal" every time I talk to you or you or I need something. You have responsibilities here at work and we all need to work as a team, which involves give-and-take. You need to learn to let things go and to give generously without always expecting something in return. I don't like working in an environment where I feel as though everything has to be negotiated and where you try to bargain with me and others. I'm not for sale. If it doesn't stop, I'm going to have to report you to our boss and to HR. So please learn to accept your assignments without having to get something from me and others in return. I appreciate your working on this and changing your behavior because your work is well done and in on time.

The Erratic One

Situation

Ernestine the Erratic One is happy one day and depressed the next. The day after that, she's angry, and the following day she is euphoric. The next day she's practically inconsolable and suicidal. Her moods are unpredictable and at times scary. You don't know what prompts her changes and you're concerned about her. You want to help her, but she doesn't listen well. She can scream at you and then a moment later she sobs. You're tired of her emotional roller coaster, and since you don't work at Six Flags, it shouldn't be your responsibility to monitor one.

Explanation

It may be possible that Ernestine is suffering from a mood disorder, possibly manic-depression also known as bipolar disorder, which is a chemical imbalance. She probably has been like this since she was younger—periods of great excitement, energy, and nonstop creativity followed by periods of sadness, crying, and lethargy interspersed with feelings of hopelessness. When she's "up," she feels fine and doesn't think she needs help. When she's low, she thinks nothing can help her and feels depressed and suicidal. If all the signs are there, and she truly does seem bipolar, then you may need to get HR involved because she needs psychological and medical assistance, which you cannot and should not provide. You need to approach her cautiously because manic-depressives usually love the productive, creative "up" cycles and don't want to lose them by going on medication. Ironically, many people suffering from bipolar disorder find that they are even *more* creative, productive, and organized when on Lithium or Depakote or alternative-medicine supplements.

Solution

Ernestine, I appreciate your strong work ethic and your dedication to your job. It's your mood swings that concern me. One day you're up and very energetic and you get a lot of work done, and the day after that, you're depressed and despondent. These ups and downs are erratic and disconcerting. I've thought a lot about you, and I'm saying this with the utmost concern about your health: please consider getting medical assistance. We have insurance that would cover it and you can also go to EAP, the Employee Assistance Program, for free. I'm telling you this because I care about you. Everybody here does. We appreciate all the hard work you do in the office and we want you to get help.

If Ernestine doesn't listen, go to HR, document all the work transgressions because of her moods swings, and let HR assist her in getting help.

The Incompetent

Situation

Ida the Incompetent may not be that bright, or she might be lazy, or maybe she's both. But she definitely is not committed to excellence in anything she does. She lets things slide, doesn't follow up, doesn't return phone calls or e-mails, lets messages slip through the cracks, and feels that work just isn't that important. She'd rather read movie magazines or cruise the Internet, learning about Britney Spears's latest escapade, Brangelina's next adoption, or what Jennifer Lopez is wearing. You feel like you're building a house on sand when you depend on her. She needs to be fired, but you can't do it. She makes everyone in the department frustrated and no one wants to work with her.

Explanation

Ida probably had parents and teachers who were negligent, didn't expect much from her, or maybe she was in remedial classes in school. She might be a "diamond in the rough" and totally capable of rising to the occasion if she had encouragement, goals, and positive reinforcement. But right now, she can't or isn't willing to do the work expected of her because she may not be qualified for her position, can't or doesn't want to ask for help, and needs the job. She may also feel like the company owes her something, so if she is doing a work slowdown, it might be her passive-aggressive revenge. If Ida is constantly dropping the ball, and it's always your mess to clean up, it's time to tell her. You have to document her costly errors, the time she takes away from you and other co-workers, and any accidents, delays, or difficulties she causes because of her gross incompetence. Most companies will not remove anyone until they realize it's costing them money, so have your proof in hand before going to your boss, your boss's boss, or HR. If it's a family-run company and Ida is a relative, the documentation is even more crucial. Attempt to get her transferred to another department to save your sanity. Find out what she likes to do and give her a job she loves where she can shine.

Solution

Ida, I appreciate that you're always here on time. We have to work together on projects, and I feel sometimes that when I depend on you, you're not delivering what I asked for. You need to become more dependable. You need to return phone calls and e-mails, find out what people want, and get your assignments completed. When you don't, it prevents me from doing my part of the project and slows down the entire department. I'd prefer to work with someone who is strong, diligent, and capable of accomplishing her assignments and goals. I need you to be more responsible, competent, and dependable. I hope you can do it. Do you think you can? If not, let's discuss what you really feel you're good at and what you love to do. Let's talk about this now so you're fulfilling your job description and your co-workers have someone to depend on.

The Chronically Late One

Situation

Constance the Chronically Late One shows up ten to sixty minutes after everyone else, without making up the missed time by cutting her lunch hour or staying late. This toxic behavior is acceptable if it only affects her, but when she starts asking you to lie for her and do her work to cover for her, you have reached the breaking point, and you must tell her you won't do it anymore.

Explanation

Sometimes a sleeping problem is to blame—the buzzer doesn't ring, the battery went dead, or there was a power outage and the clock got disconnected, but all the alarm clocks in the world won't get Constance up on time. She sets her watch ahead fifteen minutes and still is late. She may be a single mother, working two jobs, rushing to get to work, and always feeling pressured and overwhelmed. On the other hand, Constance may have ADD or ADHD—one of the symptoms is difficulty in time management. Of course there is always the chance that Constance may also be doing it to test the limits, to see just how much she can get away with, if anyone will scold her and make her adhere to the rules. You need to draw the line.

Solution

Constance, I always enjoy the conversations we have on our coffee breaks together. I have noticed that every day you arrive late for work. You walk into meetings late, and we have to catch you up on what we talked about. It's disruptive to the others who are there, and disrespectful, too. You've asked me to cover for you by saying you're in the bathroom or out getting coffee, and you've even asked me to do your work for you. I'm simply not willing to do that any longer. So please be on time in the future, and take responsibility for yourself. Your contribution to our meetings is always valued, and I'm sure it would be even more so if you arrived on time. I hope you understand. We want you on our team.

The Big-Picture Person

Situation

Bix the Big-Picture Person hates details and paperwork. He assigns them to you, and it's not in your job description. He goes on and on about how the company could grow, what it could become, and so on, yet he simply doesn't attend to his assignments at hand. Many times he doesn't meet deadlines and he's behind on his reports. When he blames you or asks you to do his work, it's time to say something and fast.

Explanation

Bix sees himself as a visionary, a guy who's leading the company on an important mission, and he doesn't have time for the little details, which, of course, can make or break a project. Bix has big plans for himself and believes he has what it takes to be company president and CEO, so he usually sees his co-workers as his servants and steppingstones. He will use you to get ahead and may give you his work to do. Don't do it. Set limits and boundaries. Let him ask the boss for an assistant if he really needs one.

Solution

Bix, I so appreciate how you have such lofty goals, and I can see how expansion into other areas can really benefit the company. There are times when I feel you're overstepping your bounds and you're doing things that aren't in your job description, trying to get me to go along with it. Or you're negligent in what is in your job description, like paperwork and follow-up, and you ask me to do your work for you. I'm not your assistant. I'm a co-worker. I feel uncomfortable in doing the detail work for your projects because I have my own projects to work on and I don't get paid to work for you. If you're interested in climbing the ladder and getting promoted, you need to discuss this with our boss and HR. There are also times when your grandiosity is at odds with reality. Thinking big is important for future goals; however, you're not the CEO and you need to focus on your job, complete your present assignments, and not stick me with the details of things that are your responsibility. I enjoy working with you and I hope we can continue, so please correct these issues I just mentioned because I'd like for us to have a cooperative working relationship here. Thanks!

The Detail Person

Situation

Denny the Detail Person is the opposite of Bix the Big-Picture Person. He gets caught up in the minutia of everything and he gets so involved in the tiniest details that he misses the big picture, his priorities, and important deadlines. He has the mind, spirit, and focus of an accountant, which is great for detail work, but it can be problematic for those who are waiting for him to hand in reports. When Denny asks you to help him with his assignments or slows down the progress of a project that your whole team is working on, it's time to confront him.

Explanation

Denny is usually an obsessive-compulsive personality and very good with details and usually with follow-up. However, sometimes he can't see the forest for the trees. He can get so involved in the small details that he can't prioritize, do what's the most important first, and finish it. He needs some perspective. If he can share his vision and focus with someone on the team like Bix, who is more big-picture-minded, they can really get projects moving. But until that happens, you have to confront Denny on how his behavior is affecting you. You might want to mention such a complementary pairing up to your boss and see if Bix and Denny would be amenable to work together, taking both of them off your hands!

Solution

Denny, I so appreciate how you are able to concentrate on the intricate details of your task and finish the research, statistics, and other data that are needed. There are times when I feel you're so involved in the little things that you fail to see your priorities and that's when the rest of us fall behind, waiting for you. We're your co-workers, not your assistants. I feel uncomfortable in doing tasks for you in our projects because I have my own stuff to work on. I suggest you partner with someone or learn how to manage your time better. So as of now, please finish your projects because I have my own work to complete. I wish you well and I know you'll be able to finish them yourself. You might also consider working with someone like Bix, who could use a detail person like you. You might make a good partnership.

The Procrastinator

Situation

Priscilla the Procrastinator puts everything off until the last minute. She can't meet deadlines, or if she does, it's only because she stays up all night finishing the work that is due the next day. She would rather do something else than prioritize what has to get done and do it. She slows down the work chain because she doesn't complete her assignments, triggering a domino effect—everyone behind her falls down. In some instances, if Priscilla's procrastination impedes the team's progress, everyone gets into trouble with the boss because the assignments aren't done when they're supposed to be.

Explanation

Priscilla the Procrastinator may be suffering from ADD or ADHD. She can find five thousand things to do other than finish her assignments. Procrastination has to do with perfectionism and fear, so Priscilla may be afraid of criticism, making a mistake, being yelled at, or failing. She may have had very critical parents who demeaned her and whom she felt she had to please and be perfect for. So she's terrified of making mistakes. She may obsess that her assignments be perfect and yet can't ever reach that goal. That's quite a burden and a great deal of pressure for anyone. Either way, her delays are frustrating you and everyone in the department.

Solution

Priscilla, I enjoy your sense of humor and I do like working with you. Your procrastination is getting to me, though, and it's causing disruption for me and the others in our department. When you miss your deadlines, you cause me and everyone here to have delays and pressure from our boss. We slow the process down for other departments and that isn't acceptable. I sense that you're a perfectionist and I admire your commitment to excellence. There's a point where it gets in your way and starts slowing things down. Maintaining a balance among excellence, productivity, and meeting deadlines without putting things off is what you should aim for. I hope you can do that because I enjoy working with you. Can I help you in any way to expedite your assignments? Would getting an assistant from the boss be useful? Let me know and I'd be happy to recommend an assistant.

The Narcissist

Situation

Norman the Narcissist is spoiled and self-centered, and he thinks the world revolves around him. He expects you and others to do his work. He is constantly talking about himself: his latest vacation, clothes purchase, celebrity sighting, or party he went to at a glamorous hot spot. He comes in late and leaves early. He takes things that are not his and feels he is better than you and everyone at work. You are tired of his stories and wasting time listening to them, and mostly you're tired of his sense of entitlement. He doesn't seem to think rules apply to him. He sees himself as management material and he sees you as his assistant. You're not, and he needs to know that.

Explanation

Norman the Narcissist is superficial and shallow and has to be the center of attention. He is consumed with money, appearances, and status. Norman doesn't have to be wealthy or come from a wealthy family to fit this description. As one of my professors said, "Narcissists don't have friends, they have fans." Norman treats all people as if they are his servants or personal assistants. Norman has little insight or introspection because it's too painful to look inside himself. Norman wants to make a lot of money, to get a trophy wife, to live in a huge mansion, and to be on magazine covers. Unfortunately, his narcissism doesn't work well while he's still stuck in a cubicle in a job where he has to cooperate with others. You need to set limits with him very quickly. If it doesn't stop, go to your boss or HR.

Solution

Norman, I appreciate that you are here on time every day. What I don't appreciate is that you seem to think you're above everyone and that you can get away with whatever you want around here. You need to stop talking about all your parties and clothes, and get down to work. I'm not your assistant, I'm your co-worker, and I'm not going to do your work for you. This is a busy office, and you're not pulling your weight around here. If you want another job, I suggest you look elsewhere because this one demands you produce. I'm not willing to cover for you or do any of your work either. So please remember that you're part of this office during the day, no matter what you've got going on outside of this job. I'd like to get along with you, so please cooperate. If you can't do your job, I'm going to go to our boss and to HR. Thanks!

The Drama Queen

Situation

Dina the Drama Queen should really be an actress. She exaggerates all her stories to larger-than-life levels, emotes like she's in a B-movie or on stage, and makes herself the center of attention. Many people live vicariously through Dina because if you were to believe her tales, she appears to live a very exciting, glamorous life. Most of the time, in reality, she's probably sitting at home watching TV while eating microwaved pizza, but to hear her tell it, she's out clubbing with multimillionaires. You seem to lead such a boring life in comparison. When she's not using the drama queen techniques to brag about her life, she employs them to exaggerate why she couldn't have her work done on time. To Dina, a broken nail is as catastrophic as being mugged or falling down a flight of stairs.

Explanation

Dina exaggerates because she feels so insecure, has low self-esteem, is terrified of abandonment, and is afraid to let people know how badly she feels about herself. She needs excitement and an adrenaline rush whenever possible. She is also very manipulative, usually tries to get her way, and get away with things. Underneath, she's a frightened, insecure child who has to embellish her very existence to make herself feel better. Her parents may have been negligent, never home, working two jobs, or traveling. When they were home, they may have spoiled her or emotionally neglected her. She grew up with a fear of abandonment and probably a lack of deep bonding, so friendships and true intimacy are things she fears yet yearns for. She's conflicted and has difficulty in friendships and in close relationships. No matter—her florid tales are interfering with you and others in the department getting work done. Dina needs a reality check and you're just the one to give it to her.

Solution

Dina, I appreciate your colorful personality. You really brighten up my day sometimes. What I don't appreciate are your excuses about why you don't have your work done. It slows all your teammates down because they depend on you to pass the next step on to them. We all have our own work to do. So please be more responsible, be on time, meet your deadlines, and get your work done. I will appreciate it and so will everyone else here at work. I know you can do it because I've seen your excellent reports before. I hope we can work well together. Thanks so much!

CHAPTER 24

The Uncommitted

The Rock Star/The Actor
The Day-Job Worker
The Sloth
The Avoider

The Uncommitted may not like their jobs, be total slackers, have hobbies, or they may just do the absolute minimum of what is expected of them, never going the extra mile. At one second after 5:00 P.M., they are out the door. Their interests, energy, and commitments lay elsewhere—their band, their night classes, their relationships, or even their second job. I'm not disparaging their need to return to school or get by on a second job, I'm talking about their *attitude*. People who are uncommitted usually work slowly, let things slip through the cracks, do the least amount of work to satisfy the boss, and leave. Or they work fast, hoping the day goes by quickly, and make mistakes because they are rushing and not paying attention. They usually don't engage in any social activities that can be avoided, and they tend to isolate themselves on the job.

I understand that people only have so much energy and if they go to school at night, or work a second job, they need to conserve their time and stamina. Uncommitted workers will make sure they have enough gas left in the tank, so to speak, to get through the next part of their day. They don't stay for long and they are prone to mistakes, incompetence, and procrastination, so they don't make good, long-term, productive employees. There is no 100 percent certain way in the interview process to figure out which potential employees are energetic, dedicated, and motivated and which ones will look at a challenging task as a hurdle to avoid. When a co-worker's behavior reveals a lack of commitment in a way that affects you, it's up to you to handle it. You may also want to alert your boss and HR about this poor work attitude, in case they are thinking of giving him or her a promotion.

The Rock Star/The Actor

Situation

Ronnie the Rock Star and Annie the Actor both feel they are gracing your business with their presence and that they really don't owe the company anything. Ronnie's in a band and Annie is waiting to go on her next audition or callback. Their "job" at your company is just a temporary gig to pay the rent. In fact, they refer to it as "my day job." Ronnie and Annie will take long lunches, especially if they have an audition. Their favorite line is, "When I'm rich and famous . . . ," although they may just be thinking it and not saying it out loud. Sometimes the Ronnies and Annies of the world do make it big and you can say, "I knew them when . . ." Rod Stewart was a grave digger, Bruce Willis worked as a bartender, and Michelle Pfeiffer worked at a supermarket, so you can make it big from any circumstances. If they have a gift and their interest lies somewhere else than their present job, then they should do everything they can to get there. Fellow workers will be better off. However, knowing that fact doesn't make it any easier to work with the superstar of tomorrow while he or she is still the office worker of today.

Explanation

Annie and Ronnie have *big* plans for their careers, but no real concern for you or your company. They are usually self-centered narcissists who have no loyalty to anyone or anything except themselves. They can be irresponsible, selfish, and constantly late because they're at acting class, an audition, or just "forgot." HR would do better to hire older, more experienced workers who come in on time, do their job well, and go home to their families. If Annie and Ronnie would just focus on the task at hand, do their job competently, and adjust their attitude for the time they are at work, it would be fine. It's the lack of attention paid that can lead to accidents, mistakes, absenteeism, and slowdowns. For whatever reasons, Annie and Ronnie are your co-workers, and you still have to deal with them. Being direct is the best route.

Solution

Annie/Ronnie, I appreciate that this company is not your life's goal and that you have other more artistic talents and ambitions. I wish you the best with those plans, and I believe in following your dreams. The reality, however, is that you are *employed here and there are certain expectations when you work here—like being on time, staying awake, and getting your assignments done, which affects me and other people in the department. If you have a late gig the night before, you still have to be on time and do your work in the morning. So please be on time and get your work in promptly. I wish you luck in your artistic career, and please let me know when you have a show or concert coming up and I will come if I can make it. I'll tell others here at the office and we can make a night of it to see you shine!*

The Day-Job Worker

Situation

Dania the Day-Job Worker is similar to the rock star in that for both, their nine-to-five job is just what they do to pay the bills. At night, they are attending night school or taking care of other obligations. Day-Job Workers are usually respectful and try their best to get their work done on time, and their attitude is one of focus and attention to the job, but because of life's challenges, they may be constantly late, absent, and missing deadlines.

Explanation

Dania may be overworked, juggling children, school, work, and even another job. People like her are doing their best, but life's circumstances may conspire to make them late for work and force them to miss deadlines. They may be barely keeping their heads above water financially and working as hard as they can to better themselves and provide for their families. It's important to have compassion for Dania and still set the limits and boundaries of what is expected of her at work.

Solution

Dania, I know that you do excellent work when you are here. I know you are going to school at night when you leave here and that you have children as well. I can understand the pressure and tight schedule you work under and I have great admiration for your ambition and your ability to juggle so many demanding tasks. I'd like to mention that sometimes you're late and you've been missing deadlines lately. It really throws me and the department off when that happens. You need to meet your deadlines. Can you do any work at home at night on your computer? What can we do to help you? Do you need an assistant? Let me know. We appreciate the good work you do here, and we want to have you in our department.

The Sloth

Situation

Steven the Sloth moves, thinks, and works slowly. The work itself, when he does it, may be good, or then again, it may not be. People who move very slowly tend to be unmotivated, and that attitude is reflected in being late for work, being unproductive, and not meeting deadlines. Eventually Steven might end up slowing down the entire office and derailing the chain of command with his slowness. If you depend on Steven's work for your deadlines, this toxic behavior is extremely frustrating.

Explanation

Steven has probably suffered from a poor self-image since his childhood. Because he is convinced of his inferiority, he never really puts in a full, honest effort at work. Steven needs to raise his self-esteem any way that he can and figure out how to get his work done in a timely manner so as to not slow down the rest of the team. Perhaps he has a physical problem—lack of energy could be from poor metabolism, adrenal impairment, a bad diet, not enough exercise, thyroid problems, overweight, cancer, depression, and/or a lack of iron, just to name a few. Perhaps a full medical check is warranted. There is probably no malicious intent on Steven's part to bring everybody down, but if he is doing so inadvertently, then it's up to you to say something. Perhaps setting a timer when he begins a project would force Steven to work faster. You need to suggest this and other tactics he can use to get moving. The boss may eventually need to have a talk with him.

Solution

Steven, I know that you can produce good work. The challenge for you is doing it on time and meeting your deadlines. I depend on your work to meet my deadlines, so when I don't get it on time, it's very frustrating for me. You must *learn to work faster. Perhaps you need some more exercise or a cardio workout to get a little extra energy each day. Perhaps you need to get a full workup from your doctor. It might be your metabolism, a lack of iron, adrenal impairment, or a low-grade depression. I'm concerned about you, and that's why I'm saying something. You have to do something, though, because your supervisor is definitely going to notice how slow you've been to get your assignments turned in, and there will definitely be consequences. It helps me to be more dynamic in my work when I set short goals and time myself to make sure that the project is coming along at a steady pace. Why don't you try integrating a new system to keep your pace in check? I know you can do it. And I hope you schedule an appointment with your physician just to make sure.*

The Avoider

Situation

Andrea the Avoider is skittish and noncommital, and she does whatever it takes to escape facing up to reality. She skirts confrontation, never stands up for herself or for anyone else, and would rather be humiliated and suffer than tell the truth and face conflict. She plays "ostrich in the sand" and believes if she doesn't deal with it, it will go away. You can never depend on her to be on your side in any confrontation. It's just too frightening for her. She is "conflict averse." When you attempt to talk to her, she always seems to have another pressing engagement to attend to all of a sudden. She can be difficult to pin down. She may appear to be shy, have a hard time looking you or anyone in the eye, and appear to have nervous habits or tics.

Explanation

Andrea the Avoider probably grew up with domineering, controling parents who scared her into meekness. Now, as an adult she still runs away from anything that has a hint of anger, acrimony, or raised voices. You must talk very softly to her, win her trust, and allay her fears. You must choose your words very carefully because if she is scared, she will either run away or close down and not listen to a word you say. I recommend taking Andrea out to lunch at a quiet restaurant where the ambiance is peaceful, with a table in the back away from people. Let the food absorb any tension. Start out with small talk and humor to break the ice. Make sure that Andrea trusts you and feels comfortable with you before you say anything to her. And do it in small increments. Focus on one or two things that you'd like her to change. If she won't talk to you, try writing her an e-mail and copying your boss. Conflict-averse people will do anything to avoid dealing with difficult or painful situations, so it may take a little extra effort to get through to them. Make sure she feels you have her best interests at heart and that you care about her. When she feels more comfortable with you, you may recommend she get into some counseling to develop more confidence and raise her self-esteem. Limited sessions at your EAP, the Employee Assistance Program, may be free, and your medical insurance may cover it.

Solution

Andrea, I enjoy working with you and you're very bright. I see that many times you avoid your responsibilities, though. In addition, you seem to just run away from anything that sounds like criticism or negative feedback and anything else that may be unpleasant. Part of life is dealing with unpleasantness, and I'd like you to develop a bit more courage so you can do so directly. When you avoid your problems, they tend to pile up and become even worse. You need to address them when they come up, and take action. Even if you're afraid, you still must deal with them. I'm here to give you support if you need it. Perhaps you should take a class on assertiveness training to help you develop more courage in speaking up. Here's a list of assertiveness books for you, and I bought this one for you as a gift. Let me know if there's anything I can do to help.

CHAPTER 25

The Angry Ones

The Fighter
The Verbal Attacker
The Threatener
The Provoker

This angry group of people is usually sitting on years of resentments, disappointments, and unmet expectations. They tend to have a very short fuse and can be explosive. Dealing with them is potentially dangerous because of their volatility. That much anger could ultimately lead to physical abuse, even in the safe-seeming world of office life. You don't want to be the target of their rages, whether verbal or physical, which is why tact, gentleness, and diplomacy are needed when you approach someone in this group. You may want or need to go to your boss or HR representative before you even attempt to deal with the person, or you may want your boss or HR to deal with him or her alone so you don't have to. Be careful when thinking of directly approaching someone in this category.

The Fighter

Situation

You may be so afraid of Phil the Fighter that you keep your mouth shut around him. He slaps his desk, he kicks the trash can, and sometimes he yells. You've heard stories that he popped a guy in the jaw once at a bar, but since it was after work and not on company property or company time, there was no disciplinary action taken against him. He seems to have a volatile temper and is always looking for a fight. You walk on eggshells around him because you have to work with him and you don't want to make him angry. Because management feels he's indispensable, they don't fire him, so it's up to you to summon the courage to safely influence his toxic behavior or have HR or your boss do it.

Explanation

Phil may have been an abused child and watched his parents fighting, yelling, and hitting each other. His first inclination when reacting to any problem is to defend himself—even if it means by fighting. People like Phil feel frightened and threatened, and because they have a short fuse, you can expect some kind of a reaction from them immediately. Phil needs to learn positive skills to control his anger and should attend anger management classes. With Phil, you should probably avoid dealing with him alone. HR should recommend this course of action to him since doing so on your own might trigger an outburst. You may need to talk to Phil with the head of HR present, or you may ask HR to do it for you, with you not even there. If you choose to do it with HR in the office, you may want to say this, or you may want HR to say something like this:

Solution

Phil, I know how competent you are and I know your reports will always be ready before the deadline. I'm very concerned about your temper, though, and I see it flare up frequently at the slightest suggestion that you made a mistake. You start yelling, and I've seen you throw things before. I don't want to be around that kind of volatile temper. Perhaps anger management courses are the solution. You have to do something to get your anger in check or I'm going to have to ask for you to be transferred to another department. People in our department are afraid of you and your temper. I would greatly appreciate it if you exercised some restraint and behaved more calmly in the future. Your work is always solid so I do hope that you get your anger under control in the future so that we can work together peacefully. Thank you!

The Verbal Attacker

Situation

Viola the Verbal Attacker believes that the best defense is a good offense and that "verbal might" makes right. Regardless of why you need to talk, Viola always has the first word and the last word, and it's always a negative remark about something you've done, or want to do, or should have done, and sometimes it's quite a stretch. She may do it to deflect any possible criticism before the fact and to disrupt incoming comments in such a way that she can control the conversation. Instead of having a productive discussion about whatever problem you're dealing with, you're now fighting to defend yourself. Viola is an expert "boomeranger," and *her* issues wind up on your lap.

Explanation

Viola probably had verbally abusive parents. Dinnertime may have been like the Harvard Debate Team or Yale Law School Moot Court—always sharpening up your verbal skills, bolstering your arguments, and strengthening your defenses. Or it could have been a way for Mom and Dad to direct their anger at each other and/or at their children. Inside, Viola may feel vulnerable, weak, and defenseless. She's lonely and scared, and she sees enemies everywhere. She doesn't trust many people, if anyone. When you confront her, you must allay her fears and stand your ground. You have to establish the rules quickly or you'll get verbally attacked again. There may be a streak of paranoia in Viola. You may end up in HR with her.

Solution

Viola, I appreciate your diligence and the work you do around here. I'd like to discuss how you lash out verbally at me and others, most of the time for no reason whatsoever or when there's the slightest hint that you've made a mistake. I find it aggressive, hostile, and unnecessary. I would appreciate it if you would stop it. I'd like you to let me finish what I have to say without interrupting me. I'm here to work with *you, not against you. We're a team and we have to work together. I respect your intelligence and I ask you to respect mine, instead of treating me and everyone else around you poorly or like we're intellectually inferior. Let's see if we can all work together, please. Thanks for your cooperation.*

The Threatener

Situation

Thad the Threatener is like Vlad the Impaler, only he does it with words instead of swords. He threatens you with a variety of tactics: going to your boss, going to HR, doing you physical harm, or whatever else he may have in his bag of intimidating tricks. He's a verbal bully and an emotional blackmailer. You are afraid of him and you walk on eggshells around him. You are afraid to report him to HR or your boss because you fear the repercussions. He also watches you like a hawk and collects infractions to be used against you—you came in ten minutes late from lunch last Tuesday, you were five minutes late to work on Monday, and so forth. You can't let him intimidate you.

Explanation

Thad compulsively has to have the upper hand. He is insecure and mean-spirited. He was probably a bully in grade school, and he likes to have people afraid of him. It's also possible he was bullied as a kid and now he seeks his revenge by bullying others. He may have had controlling, domineering parents who may have been in the military. You need to break the invisible web of fear that he has woven around you and implanted in your head. If you've done anything wrong, you have to own up to it and take the consequences. Tell your boss first so Thad can't squeal on you and get you in trouble. You need courage when confronting Thad. You have to document everything that he's done to you because he'll deny everything and claim that you're paranoid, hypersensitive, or making it all up. Be careful of him and watch your back. It may be better to confront him in the HR office with a representative there who can mediate the argument.

Solution

Thad, I think that your reports are well written and they're in on time. I'd like to work cooperatively with you. What is getting in the way, though, is your need to get your way all the time. You seem intent on frightening me and others, and trying to find out something to hold over our heads. It is very intimidating behavior, and it doesn't work with me. I'd like to know what you're so threatened about. If you have something you'd like to ask me to do, please ask it straight out without the emotional blackmail that you've used in the past. I would appreciate your honesty and not your manipulation because we have to work together. Are you willing to do that? If you aren't, then I'll have to go to our boss and to HR and tell them what you do here to me and others in the department, and trust me, they won't like it. So please work to keep your intimidation in check.

The Provoker

Situation

Prentice the Provoker does just that—he antagonizes, baits, and looks for an argument and a fight. He sets you up to take the bait and then blames you for starting the situation. He loves a good verbal debate and usually doesn't want to get physical. He just likes to argue. Sometimes he'll take the opposite viewpoint just for sport when he really agrees with you. His anger is always close to the surface so you must be careful of him. He wastes your time and energy. It needs to stop.

Explanation

Prentice probably had parents or siblings who provoked him as a child and he learned to play that game as a form of contact and a false substitute for true caring, communication, and intimacy. He likes to argue, loves drama, and does whatever it takes to manipulate an altercation into taking place. His behavior probably stems from an internal love of conflict. He may have ADD or ADHD, bores easily, and needs an adrenaline rush, so he thrives on the excitement that comes with antagonizing another person for whatever reason. He needs to vent and is looking for a target, and unfortunately, you're it. Don't bite. It's a poisonous hook and his tactics will not end well. Protect yourself and either confront him directly or go to HR with your complaints.

Solution

Prentice, I like how quickly you get your work done. What's getting in my way is how you are always trying to bait me into an argument or a fight. I've seen you do it to others as well. Some people are afraid of you and they feel like you're a pressure cooker about to explode. Not me, though. I think that we can work things out and function peacefully together in this office. We have to have an orderly work environment where people aren't afraid of each other or frightened about coming to work. If you are looking for verbal arguing, perhaps you should be a litigator and work in a courtroom or get a radio or TV talk show. But until that happens, you have to work here. It's clear that you know your job, and I like to get along with all of my co-workers, including you, so I truly hope we can work this out.

CHAPTER 26

The Politically Incorrect

The Hater

The Sexist

The Ageist

The Homophobe

The Wasteful One

The Non-PC Joke Teller

People who have prejudices are generally motivated by fear because they have had negative encounters with a few people and have generalized their experience with those people to include an entire race, class, or gender. They can be stubborn, bitter, and thoroughly indoctrinated by antiquated and hateful belief systems, usually through their parents, religious and political organizations, and social and peer groups. Education, patience, friendliness, and firm boundaries are the best tools to use with this group of people. Show them that expanding their horizons, becoming more tolerant, and being inclusive are all necessities for getting along in the modern workplace. Remember, the best teaching is by example. Sometimes the company needs to send them to diversity training and sexual harassment prevention courses again. If that doesn't work, they may need to be fired. Their behavior can be so egregious that it can result in discrimination or harassment lawsuits, people quitting, or even national media coverage. Companies should do everything they can to avoid that from happening.

The Hater

Situation

Hector the Hater is a person who talks to you about his hatred of people of different races, religions, ethnic groups, sexual orientation groups, and on and on. His speech is so negative, full of stereotypes and hate mongering, that you feel insulted hearing any of it. Hector sees everything through his own prism and dumps his prejudiced rants on you at work. By doing so, Hector is either assuming that you already agree with his wildly skewed worldview or he is trying to convert you to his way of thinking. Either way, you don't want to hear it and it interferes with your work. You find it full of hatred, prejudice, and potential violence, and you want him to stop. You have every right. You may want to go to HR to present your complaints and either have HR do it, or sit down in the HR office and confront Hector yourself. Have all your facts, quotes, and examples documented with date, time, and place as much as possible.

Explanation

Fear, distrust, and paranoia are the motivating factors for Hector and people like him. He may have grown up in a home where hate mongering or child abuse was the mode. Children usually are taught to hate. He may have been a victim of a mugging, crime, or incident with the type of person he is demeaning and he is generalizing. The trauma from his abuse or violence may still be raw. He may be needing to find a scapegoat for his problems. It may be difficult or next to impossible to change his beliefs, so it may not be worth your time to attempt to do that. What you need to do is get him to keep his mouth closed at work or there could be lawsuits. The best course of action is to tell him that his diatribes are interfering with your work and you need to concentrate. Many times the Hectors of the world are seething cauldrons of rage ready to explode, so the best thing is to not provoke them. Ask HR for help in dealing with them. Hector needs another course in diversity training to help him over his prejudices. Be very cautious when dealing with Hector. Document his transgressions when talking with him at the HR office or have HR deal with him directly. If you are going to talk to him privately, do it at a restaurant with other people present, never alone. Say something like this:

Solution

Hector, I know how you feel about certain people in the office and about people of certain races, religions, and ethnic groups in general and you have a right to your opinion. I wish you could see people in a different light because you are generalizing and there are always exceptions. However, I have work to do and I need to concentrate while I'm in the office, so I would really appreciate it if you could let me work quietly. By the way, if your rants are reported to HR, you stand being put on notice, suspended, or fired because you may be violating federal law. You might say it's your right to free speech, but others would argue that you're creating a hostile work environment. Also someone might sue you or the company for your tirades, so if I were you, I'd keep my opinions to myself while I was at work. If you value your job, you have to adhere to certain guidelines just like the company does. I hope you can do that. I'm sure you want to continue working here. Thanks for your cooperation. I appreciate it!

The Sexist

Situation

Samuel the Sexist is like Hector only his hatred is directed toward the person of the opposite sex. Samuel thinks women are stupid and conniving and use sex to get ahead. In addition to Samuel, there is Samantha, who thinks all men are controlling, abusive, brutish, and sexually predatory. These people take the dark side of gender and turn it into a generalization, attributing *all* men or *all* women to a negative category. You don't want to hear it, and it is interfering with your work.

Explanation

People like Samuel and Samantha are hurt, angry, lonely, disillusioned, and in emotional pain. They need professional help from a licensed counselor, not you. Samuel may have had a prominent female in his life (mother, girlfriend, sister, nun) who embodied all those terrible things he now feels that all women are—stupid, lazy, devious, conniving, abusive, cruel, violent, and using sex to get ahead. He's lost respect for women and is afraid of them and resents them, but he would probably never admit that. Samantha feels the same way about men based on her experiences. Both of them may be going through, or have recently gone through, a difficult breakup. They need to make the opposite sex "the bad guy" and blame them, sometimes without taking responsibility for how they may have contributed to the demise of their own marriages or relationships. On one hand, these people could deserve your sympathy because a bad experience may have led them to adopt the views they now possess. However, in a working environment, people have to put aside whatever hostilities they have in order to work together cooperatively. Anyone who appears to be incapable of doing so needs to be confronted before he or she offends someone or worse.

Solution

Sam, I know that you have certain ideas about men and women, and I find them constricting and getting in your way of seeing others clearly. I also find that some of your prejudice is directed at me without any valid reason. I know I can't change the way you feel about the opposite sex, but I'd really like to get along with you here, and since we have to work together on projects, I'd like us to cooperate with each other. Please treat me with respect from now on. I hope that we can work together to make this an amicable relationship. If you have any leftover resentment from your childhood or your divorce, you may want to take advantage of the free sessions at EAP, the Employee Assistance Program, or the low-cost counseling that our health insurance provides. It might help you calm down and resolve your issues.

The Ageist

Situation

Agnes the Ageist may resent people of any age—young children, teens, adults, or seniors—as long as it's an age removed from her own age group. Some ageists even resent people in their own age group! If her generalizations are affecting you directly in any way, then she needs to be confronted about this and learn to open her mind.

Explanation

Usually Agnes is afraid of growing old herself and it frightens her to think of the more unpleasant aspects of aging. This fear is projected out as hatred, prejudice, and discrimination. If she is prejudiced against young people, she may have forgotten how it was when she was young and starting out—the mistakes she made, her inexperience and naiveté, and her own ambition. If she's young and resentful of her own age group, she may be frightened of intimacy or friendships. Her rants are getting in the way of your work and you need to tell her before she gets herself in trouble or interrupts your work any further.

Solution

Agnes, I enjoy working with you here at the office. I hear your remarks about the younger people or older people in the office, and I'm offended. It seems you have a great deal of anger and prejudice against them and listening to it is getting in the way of my work. You might want to develop some compassion for people growing older because one day you're going to be old yourself. Perhaps that's exactly what you're afraid of. Also, the young kids in the office are learning and sometimes they make mistakes because they don't have as much experience as you do. I would recommend that you cut them both some slack and concentrate on what you have to do here at work. I'd like our work environment to be as free of negativity as possible so we can get along. You might also want to take advantage of the free sessions offered by our EAP, the Employee Assistance Program, or the low-cost counseling that our insurance offers. Thanks for listening to me.

The Homophobe

Situation

Harry the Homophobe hates gay people in the same way that Hector the Hater resents minorities, Samuel and Samantha marginalize women and men, and Agnes discriminates against certain age groups. Harry might tell offensive jokes about gay people, taunt the openly gay men and women in the workplace, and use foul epithets like *fag*, *queen*, *fairy*, or *dyke*. Whether you're gay or not, you should take offense at this behavior and know in your heart that he needs to be corrected. If your HR representative knew, he or she would probably reprimand Harry, send him to diversity training, or reprimand him. Some HR personnel would even fire him. However, if HR knew about the problem and ignored it after the victims officially complained, then the company may have a lawsuit on its hands if the gay co-workers filed a complaint or a lawsuit.

Explanation

Harry is a frightened and a possibly repressed person. Perhaps he was sexually molested as a young boy and still has disturbing memories of it. Perhaps he represses his own gay issues and is actually in the closet. Or he may be a macho or religious person who thinks being gay is sick, perverted, or wrong. He may feel threatened or even secretly attracted, which he probably would never admit. Either way, he needs to keep his opinions to himself at the workplace and get on with his assignments. You might be able to bring some understanding and compassion to his world. Whether or not he wants to change, he needs to concentrate on his duties, keep his mouth closed with his homophobic remarks, and not offend anyone. You can diplomatically inform him that he needs to stop this behavior. If he continues and it is reported to HR and he still doesn't stop, then someone can sue the company for not taking action and creating a hostile work environment. Companies need to do everything they can through education and discipline to prevent such lawsuits.

Solution

Harry, I enjoy working with you and I admire your tenacity in getting all the work done here on time. I hear your remarks about gays in the office, though, and I don't care for that kind of talk at all. It seems you have a great deal of anger and prejudice against gays and listening to it is getting in the way of my work and creating an atmosphere of tension around the office. You might want to develop some understanding about what it means to be gay and review the diversity training materials from the class that we took. Even if you don't change the way you feel, you should at least keep your opinions to yourself to make this a comfortable work environment. I'd like to work in a place free of negativity and I hope you will comply. I'm sure you wouldn't want to be the cause of a lawsuit against the company. I hope you understand that I'm saying this to help you. Thanks so much!

The Wasteful One

Situation

Wendell the Wasteful One throws away things that are recyclable, he doesn't shake the toner cartridge to use it to the very last drop, and he prints out e-mails when he could save them in his computer and make a backup copy on his thumb drive. He wastes supplies, is too lazy to recycle, and may believe that global warming is a hoax.

Explanation

Wendell doesn't comply with the green agenda on the planet. He may not believe in global warming or is just too lazy to care about the environment and any company-wide initiatives to clean it up. HR usually provides training for people to learn to recycle bottles, glass, plastic, aluminum, and paper; save files and e-mails in the computer and thumb drive instead of printing them out; and save gasoline by carpooling, taking the bus, and other cost- and fuel-saving measures promoted by most companies. You can be a good role model for Wendell and for others in your office: if your company doesn't have recycling bins in the lunchroom, then tell HR to put them in and monitor it yourself. Take responsibility to contribute to the betterment of the planet, and be sure to confront Wendell only if he's being deliberately wasteful and flouting company policy about the environment. The best teaching is by example. Sometimes educating someone turns them into an advocate for the cause.

Solution

Wendell, I think that you're a great worker and I have enjoyed the conversations we have had when we were both stuck working on projects past 5:00 P.M. I have to say, though, that in this age of recycling, I'd like you to be more aware of how we can all save around the office. We have recycling bins set up in the lunchroom for glass, paper, aluminum, and plastic, and I have noticed that you don't seem to use them. Also, you can save e-mails into your computer, put them on a thumb drive, and save paper by not printing them out. Regardless of your ideas about global warming, recycling can help the planet save its natural resources and I do hope you'll comply. We're all conscious of recycling here and we're all doing our best to carpool and save our resources. I'd like you to be aware of it and join the effort here at work and even when you're home. Thanks!

The Non-PC Joke Teller

Situation

Joey the Non-PC Joke Teller can come in four categories: (1) one who is clueless about what he's saying as he verbally insults all demographics of people with his inappropriate jokes; (2) one who deliberately tells off-color, racist, misogynistic, and homophobic jokes to insult people, stir the pot, and be mean-spirited; (3) one who tries to alleviate office tension by telling jokes, which turn out to be politically incorrect and ironically, only increases the anxiety and tension; and (4) one who is practicing his stand-up routines for the local comedy clubs and wants your feedback. Whatever Joey's motivation, you feel uncomfortable when he starts, and so do others. It is inappropriate for the workplace. He needs to be told this and to stop it. Joey is a lawsuit waiting to happen.

Explanation

Joey may be harboring deep-seated resentment and prejudice against certain races, ethnic groups, religions, women, and gays based on negative experience from his parents, childhood, teen years, or adulthood. He may have been beaten up, threatened, or bullied by certain people and turned that into hatred. He may also just really like the attention that comes from telling "shocking" jokes. Whatever the case may be, Joey is projecting his anger and resentment onto others. He uses "humor" to cover his insults. When you call him on it, he says, "What's the matter? Can't you take a joke?" or "You're so sensitive. Get over it!" or "I was only joking! You're a stiff. Relax."

The first step should always be confronting the offending person directly and privately. You need to pull Joey aside in another room, outside, or at lunch, because if you do it in front of others, you're giving him the audience he craves and he will turn his "humor" on you to embarrass, humiliate, and degrade you in front of co-workers. If confronting him doesn't work, get his boss or HR involved. Joey, most likely, will refuse to accept responsibility for his behavior, and he'll try to blame you for "ratting him out," so you need to document everything—where and when you heard every tasteless and insulting joke he has ever told in your presence. If you can get any other co-workers to do the same and act as witnesses, you'll have strength and power in numbers when you report it to the boss and to HR. They need documentation to discipline him and you can provide that.

Solution

Joey, you have a gift as a comic and you should really pursue open-mike nights at a comedy club in your spare time. It's your choice of material here at work that I find offensive and inappropriate at the office, though. I find that your insulting jokes are really tasteless, cruel, and mean-spirited. I hope your humor isn't deliberately pointed this way; even if it is, that's not cool. You are jeopardizing the company, which might be sued because of your behavior if anyone else is as offended as I am. If HR finds out or someone reports you to them, you will get disciplined and maybe even get fired. You need to stop now and I ask you to do so before you get fired. I hope you can clean up your material when you're here at the office because you may have a career as a comedian or comedy writer, and if so, you might learn to be funny without offending people. Either way, you definitely have a reason now to make your humor less offensive, so please do. Thanks!

CHAPTER 27

The Victims

The Fearful One

The Delicate Flower

The Victim

The Martyr

The Whiner

The Crybaby

The Chaos Creator

The Money Borrower

The Victims have erroneously learned from their parents, teachers, siblings, and others during their childhood that they have no power, can't change anything, and shouldn't speak up and voice their concerns. They see themselves as innocent bystanders and victims who can't help but roll over when people who are more powerful want to mow them down and use them. Since childhood they have become a bundle of neurotic and sometimes contradictory traits—demanding of attention, passive, frightened, and yet not owning their power. They can guilt-trip you, make you feel like their problems are your fault, and make you feel responsible for rescuing them. None of that is true nor is it your duty or obligation to make good on their version of reality. They can set you up to take advantage of them and then blame you. They play a huge game of "lose/lose" or "lose/win" having to be the victim. So they "win" by "losing." Many of them are clever manipulators and some are totally unaware of the games they play. They can be very frustrating to deal with, to say the least. You need to call a process shot on what they do and how they set you up. Be vigilant to not allow them to victimize you or themselves. You need to be on your toes with this group of people at all times and be assertive in your dealings with them, pointing out how, where, and when they do what they do. Some sincerely may want to change their behavior and would make good candidates for therapy, which you can recommend. Others have no desire to stop playing the toxic games of victimhood, so beware and be aware!

The Fearful One

Situation

Fern the Fearful One is always scared: of being fired, yelled at, disliked—you name it! Fern is always walking on eggshells. She's hypervigilant, and her anxiety makes you nervous. She is like Andrea the Avoider in many ways. You can usually not depend on her to back you up on anything—documenting a co-worker's abuse, standing up to a rude boss, or going to HR to report someone. She is terrified of confrontation, criticism, or taking a risk of any kind. Fern is usually shy, has low self-esteem, and doesn't believe in herself; she is frightened of growing, expanding her skills, going back to school, or anything that demands that she face her fears. With the proper encouragement, counseling, and emotional support, Fern truly has the potential to grow and turn from a caterpillar into a beautiful butterfly.

Explanation

Fern may have had parents who grew up during the Depression or went through very difficult times. She absorbed their fear throughout her childhood, so everything she does is colored by anxiety. Fern may also be living on a tight budget or have a great many burdens and responsibilities, like taking care of her aging parents, children, or grandchildren, so she is fearful of taking any risks. She usually doesn't disclose personal information to others out of a deep, abiding shyness. She usually won't stand up for herself or anyone else because she's so afraid of losing her job, even when it's clear that she is in the right. She can be a sweet and thoughtful person. It's just that her fears paralyze her. She can grow and change with counseling, friendship, and emotional support. If you want to take on an Extreme Makeover, then Fern's your gal.

Solution

Fern, I am so glad we work together because you are very considerate. I know you're frightened of things and I can understand your anxiety. It's important to address your issues when they come up and to take action. It's OK to be scared about some things; however, you still must deal with them. When you are fearful to the point of an anxiety attack every time something unpleasant comes your way, it makes me nervous, and I don't like to feel that way unless I absolutely have to. I know you have it within you to face the challenges that come your way on the job, and I can't wait to see you stand your ground like I know you can. I'm here to give you support if you need it. You might want to take advantage of the free sessions from EAP, the Employee Assistance Program, or get into counseling that our insurance pays the bulk of to help free you of your fear and anxiety. You're a sweet person and I'd like to see you relax more, have greater self-esteem, feel more confident to expand and take more risks. I know you can do it.

The Delicate Flower

Situation

Debbie the Delicate Flower is allergic to just about everything—perfume, aftershave, dust mites, chalk, pesticides, cleaning solutions, loud noises, and even fluorescent lighting, just to name a few. You must always be very careful around her, and she probably has asked you to stop wearing perfume/aftershave, to not talk loudly, and to turn off your office fluorescents. Debbie should probably work from home where she can control her own environment more to protect her sensitivities. She would probably prefer to work in a clean, sterile environment like "the boy in the bubble," if it were possible. It's difficult to work with Debbie because so much of your normal behavior is restricted since you don't want to set off her sneezing spell or send her to the hospital with an allergy attack. If HR allows it, perhaps Debbie can work from home. That might be an option to pursue. Or Debbie might be isolated to an area out of the way of offending odors, lights, and irritants. She may be an excellent worker or miss work because of her infirmities and sensitivities. Creative solutions might be best to maximize Debbie's effectiveness in her work environment, like working from home or a separate office out of the way.

Explanation

There are some people who are just born with delicate, hypersensitive systems. Debbie the Delicate Flower is probably one of them. She may have serious allergies and she may be on prescription or over-the-counter medication to combat them. If she is, it sounds like the remedies are not working. Debbie may not even want to get better because she may be a hypochondriac who gets "secondary gain" from her ailments—she complains, looks like the long-suffering martyr, and uses her sensitivity as a convenient excuse for not doing work, coming in late, leaving early, or any other way that sickness earns her a pass. It's frustrating to work with Debbie, as nice as she may be, and you need to confront her or go to HR if the problems start to get out of hand. If she has "secondary gains" in staying sick, as mentioned above, then the boss or HR needs to take constructive and creative action to empower Debbie to get help from an allergist, nutritionist, alternative medicine physician, chiropractor, acupuncturist, or medical doctor to help alleviate or rid her of the allergies and cope better with a working environment. Otherwise, a home office might be the best place for Debbie.

Solution

Debbie, I have noticed that you seem to have serious allergies in this work environment. I understand sensitivities to light, sound, pesticides, odors, fragrances, cleaning solutions, and other substances. Have you seen an allergist, a chiropractor, acupuncturist, a holistic practictioner, or an alternative medicine doctor? It might help get rid of the things that bother your system. I must say it must be quite frustrating for you. It also seems as though some-

times you use your allergies as excuses for getting your work in late, missing deadlines, coming in late, or leaving early. That's when your allergies get in the way of your work and productivity here. More important, though, I don't appreciate how much you expect us all to alter the way we work and the environment we work in just to accommodate you. I don't mind making a few changes to prevent your allergies from acting up, but when you add your noise complaints and other requests into the mix, it becomes a bit too much for a normal office. Please do what you can to meet me halfway by being a little more tolerant in general. Or if you find working from home is a more protected environment for you, please contact the boss who may allow you to do that. I recommend that you pursue that as a viable possibility. See what the company can do. You're a great co-worker in every other respect, so there's no reason we can't get along well. Thanks for listening to me. I hope we can work out a solution here that can accommodate you and if not, working from home might be an excellent alternative for you.

The Victim

Situation

Vicki the Victim seems to get into trouble no matter what she does. Tragedy has a way of striking her on a daily basis as though she were a magnet for disaster. When she doesn't get her work done, it's never her fault; it's because "things just happen" to her. Vicki also tells you all her problems—of which there are plenty—even though it's not in your job description to listen to them. You have work to do and you're not licensed to be Vicki's counselor or psychotherapist. Her problems seem endless. Like the Hydra, if one problem is "cut off" and solved, two others rise to take its place. It's exhausting to be around Vicki the Victim because she sucks the energy right out of you and gives nothing back. She's a taker, not a giver—but you don't have to take it anymore.

Explanation

Vicki gets attention for being a victim. She creates this perception of herself by attracting all sorts of mishaps, bad boyfriends, and financial problems with her poor attitude so she can have people feel sorry for her. She then uses these situations as excuses for why she can't get her work done. It's a vicious circle and one that she feels hopeless about and powerless to change. Vicki probably had a chaotic childhood, filled with parents who were constantly struggling with poverty, drug addiction, alcoholism, domestic violence, child abuse, police raids, and/or other traumatic events. Crises and chaos were and are her daily diet, and she believes that tempo is "normal"; so even when nothing is happening, she consciously or unconsciously creates havoc so she can feel "safe" in a familiar environment. She could benefit from individual and group psychotherapy, so giving her information about EAP, the Employee Assistance Program, and approved providers information from your insurance carrier might be helpful. Let her know how her issues are affecting you, and politely ask her to make some changes.

Solution

Vicki, I know you do a good job here, and I'm flattered that you feel comfortable talking to me. I need to tell you, though, that I find it rather difficult to concentrate on my duties whenever you come to my desk to talk. If you just wanted to have a quick chat, I wouldn't mind, but it seems like you just want to list an entire litany of your problems with people who take advantage of you. A conversation is supposed to go two ways, and I don't feel like that is what happens when we talk. You seem to almost relish it when bad things happen to you, and it's hard for me to hold my tongue every time you tell me another victim story. Therapy might help you. Your life's troubles seem overwhelming, and I'm on overload when you tell me even one of them—no less three or four. In life, you get what you put up with, Vicki. You seem to almost like *being a victim because it serves as an excuse for not finishing your work. A positive attitude makes a big difference. If you would take what I've said into consideration and only talk to me when you want to have an actual dialogue about work, I'm sure we can continue to coexist here peacefully in the office. Thanks so much!*

The Martyr

Situation

Mildred the Martyr probably was raised by martyrs just like her, who may have grown up during the Depression or during hard times, or people who are "doing their duty" with no real love in their hearts. She takes on more than she has to and always lets you know it. She may tell you how much work she has to do, how little sleep she's gotten, how hard she has worked, and how no one appreciates her, or she may suffer in silence with her measured sighs, exasperated eye rolling, weighted shoulder shugging, and overburdened body language. She wants to be nominated for sainthood and canonized, so she continues to take on other people's work even though she knows it's not her responsibility. She's always willing to do the work, but she resents it, doesn't usually do it with a good heart, and makes you know exactly that—you're putting another load on her, but "it's all right, I don't mind." You can cut the tension with a knife. She lays a guilt trip on you that is so onerous and oppressive that you feel as though Mildred's plight is yours and that you have to rescue her or that you feel like a slacker compared with her. Then it dawns on you that you resent it and resent her, which is what a guilt trip really is.

Explanation

Mildred believes and likes to feel as if she's getting the short end of the stick and she sets it up like that to happen. It confirms her sense of low self-esteem, unworthiness, and being trapped. She wants recognition, acknowledgment, and approval for being a martyr because she doesn't know any other way to get those needs met. People may take advantage of her and give her their work to do, which she'll take on willingly, suffering in silence or making martyred comments to let you know she's overburdened. She doesn't know how to say no, and even if she did, she wouldn't want to. It's her identity, her cause, and her raison d'être. What people don't seem to really grasp is how strong, tenacious, and persistent martyrs really are, even though they look weak and helpless.

Solution

If you see others doing it to her, you can say:

Mildred, I think you're excellent at your job, and I've noticed how everyone piles their work on you and you seem to willingly take on the extra burden whether you can handle it or not. You know that you don't have to do that. It's not fair for other people to subcontract their work out to you without giv-

ing you any credit or extra pay in return. You don't have to do it and you should be assertive and say no. You need to have some fun and let loose a little bit. Why don't we go out to dinner after work and go see a movie?

If she's doing it to you, you need to call a process shot on her, make her own her own choices, and take responsibility for her decisions:

Mildred, I asked you if you could do this and you said sure. However, your body language and your nonverbal communication are telling me that you really resent it and are playing martyr. I don't need a guilt trip, and I asked you to affirm that you could and that you have the time. I'd be happy to pay you for it, and if that works for you, great. And I don't want you doing it and then laying a martyr trip on me like I'm burdening you. So make a choice: tell me if you can do it and I'll pay you for it, or tell me you can't do it because you don't have the time. The choice is yours.

The Whiner

Situation

Wendy the Whiner sounds like a baby endlessly complaining about everything—she can't do something, she's powerless, she doesn't know how, she doesn't have the right supplies, and the list goes on. Wendy brings her personal problems to work and constantly complains about her home and family, her sex life, and work problems, but she never does anything to change them because she craves the attention and pity—bring out the Kleenex! You want to say to her, "Do you want cheese with that whine?" She is also an excuse machine and plays "Yes, but . . ." with you constantly. You give her suggestions and she negates each one with "Yes, but I can't because . . ." It's a no-win situation for you, so don't even get started giving her helpful suggestions. She doesn't want them. She'd rather complain, feel helpless and sorry for herself, and stay stuck. She's depressed, unhappy, and weak, and she has unfathomable depths of disappointment, resentment, and hidden rage. You've got to confront her with this or you'll never get a moment of peace or any work done. Call a process on Wendy the Whiner like you did with Mildred the Martyr.

Explanation

Wendy is usually codependent, feels helpless and hopeless, and doesn't know how to get out of her rut. Whining is really powerless anger with nowhere to go because whiners don't think that they have the right to be angry, direct, and confrontational, so they transform it into whining, which is like nails on a blackboard. Short of giving Wendy the number of a qualified psychotherapist, there isn't much you can do to help her feel better about herself. What you can do is ask her to change the way she expresses her feelings while she's on the clock and in the workplace because it drives you and everyone else crazy. Call a process shot on her—get Wendy to take responsibility for her own anger and be assertive about why she's upset, with whom, and what she'd like for the ideal outcome. That way she can stop the whining, be emotionally honest, and be direct.

Solution

Wendy, your organizational skills are exceptional and you really do good work. Your co-workers and I find your whining and complaining about your personal problems to be a negative influence on our way of working. You sound powerless, hopeless, and weak. Knowing you, I think that isn't the full story. You like to complain and blame other people for your circumstances. We have free limited sessions at our Employee Assistance Program, and our insurance covers psychotherapy and counseling with a very small co-pay. Perhaps you can find a counselor and deal with your issues with a professional in a private office instead of bringing your troubles to work and discussing them with your co-workers. There may be a lot of things troubling you that are getting in the way of your work and relationships here at the office. Perhaps if you talked about some more pleasant topics than the problems themselves, you might feel better about everything. I'd feel better, too, if you stopped complaining about everything. Remember that you're in the driver's seat of your life, and you have control over all these things that you seem to feel powerless about now. You need to own your own power, look at your choices, and stop whining. I wish you good luck and I know this is the best advice I can give you at this time.

The Crybaby

Situation

Cathy the Crybaby is similar to Wendy the Whiner with the added feature that she uses tears to get her way and turns on the waterworks for effect. Sometimes this works—some people simply buckle when confronted with a crying woman—so Cathy has learned that crying is a viable tactic. It lets her off the hook and gets her what she wants.

Explanation

Many men buckle at a crying woman and give in. Perhaps Cathy learned this tactic at her grandfather's or father's knee and she has used it ever since to get her way. Cathy may be stuck in some form of arrested development where she still relies on the same tactics that she used as a child with her parents or grandparents to deal with the rest of the world as an adult. If you're someone who can't deal with a crying woman, then you have to learn to be strong and confront her if and when you need to. You don't want to be the bad guy; you want to help her, so you're torn. The best thing you can do for Cathy is show her that using tears as a defensive weapon isn't always going to work. Remember, you're doing Cathy a favor by showing her ways to be assertive and own her power, rather than cry, whine, manipulate, and drive people crazy.

Solution

Cathy, I always admire the work you turn in. You are a very capable employee. It seems, though, like you sometimes use tears to either make me feel sorry for you or to get your way at crunch time. Maybe you don't even realize that you cry so often, but I can think of many instances when you've done so in the past month. Maybe you think that men will let you have your way if you cry, and some men will relent, but many resent it, as do women. Regardless of whether it's intentional or not, this crying to get your way has got to stop. Not everybody is going to give you a free pass in this world just because you shed some tears, Cathy, and I'm being honest with you. When you use tears to get sympathy, you are disowning and rejecting the power you have. You can regain that personal power by being assertive and saying exactly what you need and want. You can also talk about whatever is trou-

bling you and getting in the way of your work and relationships here at the office. You can feel like you're in the driver's seat of your life instead of like a powerless victim. I hope you'll take my advice because you're a good worker and I'd like to see you succeed on your own terms without resorting to crying. I know you can do it!

The Chaos Creator

Situation

Carrie the Chaos Creator is like Vicki the Victim, except Carrie has more energy and is not as passive as Vicki. Carrie finds herself constantly amid turmoil, and her life is one struggle after another. Carrie, like Vicki, probably had a chaotic childhood, filled with parents who were constantly struggling with poverty, drug addiction, alcoholism, domestic violence, child abuse, police raids, or other traumatic events. Crises and chaos were and are her daily diet, and she believes that tempo is "normal"; so even when nothing is happening, she consciously or unconsciously creates havoc so she can feel "safe" in a familiar environment. Carrie always has a personal crisis preventing her from being on time and doing her work—car trouble, children's illnesses, house disasters, a spouse leaving, AWOL babysitters—it doesn't matter. She uses all of these as excuses to not get her work done. And it's always something, isn't it? All the mechanics, plumbers, counselors, and doctors in the world couldn't solve her problems! When she stops this pattern, the good news is that even though she may be a procrastinator, she usually works well under deadlines.

Explanation

Carrie loves excitement, crises, danger, and suspense because it generates adrenaline, which gives her a lift physiologically and psychologically. She can't live without drama, so if none is to be found, she will create it, consciously or unconsciously. She is probably a codependent personality who needs a crisis to feel alive, useful, and important. She may be a functional chaos creator who gets her work done on time, but she may be an unproductive type who doesn't get any work done on time at all. To prevent her from creating her parade of distractions, getting in your way, delaying your deadlines, or interfering in your productivity, you must set the limits and monitor her progress. Otherwise, there will always be some chaotic occurrence that enables her to miss the deadline.

Solution

Carrie, when you're here and focused, your output is impressive. However, I've noticed that you've been late for work three or four times a week because of one crisis or another. There always seems to be an obstacle of some sort that prevents you from getting here on time. It's like you need these crises to feel alive or important, or this is familiar territory from your childhood. It's got to stop or you could be in danger of being fired. Make a list of babysitters, plumbers, car mechanics, and doctors who are near your home. There's an old saying that chance favors the prepared. If you take some precautions to fortify yourself against any impending crises, then you just may be able to ward them off before they happen. In any case, we really need you to get here at 9:00 and get your work done. I like it when your work is finished on time because your reports are comprehensive. I hope we can work well together from now on.

The Money Borrower

Situation

Monty the Money Borrower constantly hits you up to borrow five dollars, never pays you back, and by now, he probably owes you several hundred dollars. Yet he always has an excuse as to why he can't pay you back and why he needs to borrow even more money. You resent it and find yourself avoiding him because you're tired of being his ATM.

Explanation

Monty the Money Borrower needs a class in budgeting, finances, and checkbook balancing. He should be put on an allowance and have his credit cards taken away. He may have a gambling problem or overwhelming debts, or he may just be a terrible money manager. On the other hand, he could be a manipulative sort who counts on you not remembering that you lent out an "insignificant" sum like five dollars. That money adds up after a while, though, and so you have to put your foot down and not lend Monty money anymore. What's more, you have to stand up for yourself and confront him directly if you want to get back the money he owes you.

Solution

Monty, I enjoy working with you. I look forward to hearing your next funny joke. However, I find that you're constantly asking me for money to borrow, and it has gone too far. Do you think I've forgotten about all the times I've lent you five dollars? I really don't want to be in the position I'm in right now—having to ask for my own money back—but you've driven me to this. I will not lend you any more money and you need to pay me back in full what you owe. You're an intelligent person—you just need to clean up your act when it comes to money. I expect to be paid in full by next month, Monty. That's plenty of time for you to figure out how you'll budget the money. I wish you the best in learning to be a better money manager. If I don't get the money back in full, I'm going to report this to HR.

CHAPTER 28

The Rescuers

The Arranger
The Problem Solver
The Mother Hen

The Rescuers are always looking for people to help, office fires to put out, and problems to solve, which may be thoughtful and exactly what is called for, that is, until the negative part of their "rescuing" comes to the surface: their need to always be right and to make themselves indispensable. They consciously or unconsciously work to make you and others dependent on them, and they just take over and dominate a situation when you don't need rescuing. They need to be needed and can be very dependent and codependent personalities themselves, although they always look like the strong, capable, helpful rescuer. When you find them practically creating problems or yelling like Chicken Little that the sky is falling just so they can rush in like a superhero and save the day, you know you have to put your foot down, set limits, and not get involved with them. They can attach themselves to you and to a department like a blood-sucking leech and not let go. Set limits, be tactful and firm, and avoid letting them do "nice" things for you by not giving them any power over you, because there's always a catch. Strings are attached to their "giving"; and it's not strings—it's cables.

The Arranger

Situation

Alice the Arranger thinks she's the social director of the office and has taken it upon herself to keep everyone's dance card full. She is the self-appointed office arranger—evenings out, birthday parties, lunches, collecting for gifts, sending flowers to the new mother, and so on. Alice might be performing really useful, kind deeds, but her superior attitude can be annoying, especially when combined with the fact that making arrangements seems to be a full-time job for her. When does she do her real job? She always seems to be coming around, asking you to join this group, contribute to this cause, attend the next function, often asking for donations at inappropriate times and taking *pesky* to a new level. Perhaps you and other co-workers just want to be left alone or to just contribute money and not attend every social function she arranges.

Explanation

Alice needs to feel wanted and included. The only surefire way she has devised for always being a member of the group is to take charge and run the group herself. She loves for things to be orderly and planned, and so making arrangements is a good outlet for her in this regard. If she were a wedding planner or worked specifically as the company's events planner, she might be a lot happier, finally able to put her tremendous organizational and networking skills to full use and power. So she does what she does best as an extra "hobby" at work. It can be wonderful sometimes, having certain activities planned and coordinated, but unfortunately many times it ends up being annoying as you are interrupted yet again to contribute for flowers and sign a card for "Marty from Accounting," whom you barely even know. When it gets to the annoying stage, it's time to say something. Be cautious because many times the Alices of the world, who care so much about others and want to be acknowledged and accepted, can be hypersensitive to rejection and very thin-skinned. Be sure to carefully word your discussion with her to not hurt her feelings.

Solution

Alice, I admire your organizational abilities and how you can pull order out of chaos. Your networking, kindness, thoughtfulness, and thoroughness are exemplary, and the office is a better place for what you've done. What I find is that some people aren't quite as social as you, and they don't want to keep stopping what they're doing to donate time and money toward everything that comes up. Perhaps I'd like to send a card by myself, and I'd like you to send me one e-mail and let me make up my own mind about how I'd like to respond or contribute. I appreciate everything you do around here, so one e-mail is fine for me. Thanks so much! I hope you understand and thanks again for being so thoughtful and caring about everyone who works here. I really appreciate it and so do others!

The Problem Solver

Situation

Penny the Problem Solver is the "go to" person in the office for any business-related difficulties. She makes herself indispensable as a fountain of knowledge and information, which is a beneficial service of course. That is, until one day you realize that you've come to depend on her for everything. You've gotten so used to having Penny help you in crucial moments that you realize you wouldn't know what to do if certain problems were to occur when she's not there. Less likely, but also a potential problem, she might simply refuse to give you the information one day, under the guise of not having it, when it's clear from experience that she does. Playing subtle passive-aggressive games and withholding information is also in her basket of tricks and is a way for her to wield power over others.

Explanation

Penny likes to be in control, and in her role as office problem solver, she gets to do so under the guise of "knowing what's best" or "helping out." What she is really doing is absorbing your power and making you dependent on her. On the one hand, she is "helping" you, but there are strings attached. Problem Solvers are great for a while—until people start relying on them and they get overloaded, as they always do. Then everything can fall apart with disastrous consequences for the business. Problem Solvers tend to become secret keepers, too, by hoarding power, information, and statistics from other co-workers. They will say, "Oh, I'll take care of that. Don't worry about it. No problem. Consider it done." Then something doesn't get taken care of and who gets the blame? The Problem Solvers? No, they were "just trying to help." The person who has his or her head on the chopping block is the one who was assigned the task in the first place. Be aware of Penny's hidden motives and don't get caught up in her web. She likes to keep the scales unbalanced so she can call in favors or guilt-trip you about how much she's done for you. You need to be as independent as possible, develop your own problem-solving skills and databases, and not give your power away to Penny, who can abuse that position. Remember, for information you have a little resource called the Internet.

Solution

Penny, I really appreciate how you offer to help everyone here, including me, when we need help. Sometimes it almost seems as though you don't want people to know how to do things on their own. I remember last week when I asked you how to process that report, you said you'd take care of it. I didn't want you to take care of it, though—I wanted to take care of it myself. I understand that you're not always going to be available to help me out. In the future, if I need help with something, do you think you could show me how to do it so I could handle it by myself? I don't want to have to keep bugging you because I know you have a lot on your plate and also because I value my independence. I hope you will take what I've said into consideration because I do enjoy working with you. Thanks for listening.

The Mother Hen

Situation

Molly the Mother Hen takes care of everyone in the office as if each co-worker were her child and she was the concerned mother. She bakes muffins, remembers everyone's birthday with a card and a gift, always asks how your children are doing, how your mother's health is, and how your father's broken hip is healing. She is like Alice the Arranger, but on a more personal level with each individual at the office.

Explanation

Molly the Mother Hen is a very concerned, loving, and nurturing person. Her caring for others is usually sincere, touching, and kind in most cases, and she may have done this with her own children; or she may not have any children at all and does this to satisfy her maternal urges. But the dark side to Molly is that she can be a "smother mother." She needs to be needed and she has a difficult time in letting go; she can be controlling, likes to know every piece of personal information about you, and has a difficult time when people disagree with her or try to emerge from under her wing. She can ask very personal questions and somehow she feels that she's entitled to the information for all the "caring" that she shows you. Many people chafe at her concern, becoming skeptical and distrustful of it the more it's felt. Molly needs to learn that caring isn't about controlling. Compliment her on her thoughtfulness and what a nice touch she brings to the office, while stating where she may have stepped over social boundaries by being too intrusive.

Solution

Molly, I so appreciate your thoughtfulness on my birthday and your delicious blueberry muffins. I find your kindness so sweet and genuine and I'm touched by it. Sometimes you ask very personal questions, though, and you do so in front of others. It feels a little intrusive when you do that, and I'd like to protect my privacy and still have you as a cherished colleague. I hope you understand and we can continue being friends. Thank you so much for all the kind things you do for me and for others in the office, and I hope that you will respect my privacy. I appreciate it!

CHAPTER 29

The Saboteurs

The Passive-Aggressive

The Silent Treatment

The Sugarcoater

The Smiling Cobra

The Thief

The Idea and Credit Stealer

The Naysayer

The Envious One

The Practical Joker

Saboteurs can be deceitful, malicious, and even sociopathic. They are the office villains, and they seem to embrace the role. They're the ones pretending to be your friend while stabbing you in the back, grinning and making promises they have absolutely no intention of keeping, telling you one thing and doing something else. They can be deliberate and methodical in their plotting or spontaneous and spur-of-the-moment in their misdeeds. When you confront them, they may lie or deny what they've done, making a show of protesting that they are blameless and how could you accuse them of such behavior. You must vigilantly guard against the Saboteurs and document everything with e-mails, phone logs, and letters. Be very careful in dealing with this group. Some of them have characteristics of a sociopathic or psychopathic personality, also referred to as the antisocial personality in the *Diagnostic and Statistical Manual of Mental Disorders*, or *DSM IV*, published by the American Psychiatric Association.

The Passive-Aggressive

Situation

Pam the Passive-Aggressive is sneaky, devious, and deliberate, but she pretends that everything happens by accident. She always seems to "forget" what is inappropriate to mention or the fact that she promised to help and didn't or that the deadline of an assignment has passed. She insists that she is innocent, though. Don't be fooled by the innocent façade. Pam may seem sweet, but she does nasty things to you behind your back or even to your face, like "forgetting" to tell you that you had a phone call or that an important package came in, or that the urgent overnight delivery you've been waiting for has been sitting on her desk for hours. That type of passive-aggressive behavior is harder to address than outright hostility because she is covered from guilt by the cloak of supposed forgetfulness. No matter how difficult it may be to face her about it, if this toxic behavior is giving you grief, then you must confront it. If not, it will just get worse.

Explanation

Pam is a very angry person inside and usually had controlling, rigid, and self-righteous parents who conditioned her to keep her anger repressed. This outlook could have been reinforced by her teachers, religion, and even friends. So to remain sane, Pam has taken her anger underneath the surface and figured out how to express it in passive ways. Calling a process shot on Pam is the most effective tactic to combat her passive-aggressiveness—doing aggressive, nasty things in a passive manner. She needs to be confronted about this behavior because she thinks you don't know it when she does something nasty. You must inform her that you'd rather have her voice her discontent to you than quietly sabotage you with her actions. Then you should give her the space to be assertive, which may be scary for her, given her programming. Passive-aggressive people, whether male or female, are very frustrating to deal with. An excellent book on this subject is *Living with the Passive Aggressive Man*, by Scott Wetzler, Ph.D.

Solution

Pam, I know that you're a very competent worker and I appreciate that about you. I see that sometimes you seem angry or upset, but you try not to let it show outwardly. You seem to do nasty things under the guise of "forgetting," and your withholding information—like not telling me the urgent package arrived—feels like spite and revenge. Yet I have no idea what I've done to earn your enmity. It feels as though you're not being emotionally honest and up front with me. Even if you have a smile on your face, I can tell by your behavior that you're upset with me—and that creates an air of tension in this office. If you're angry at me, please tell me directly what I did so we can have a discussion about it and resolve it. I'd like to work cooperatively with you and I hope we can do that in the future.

The Silent Treatment

Situation

Cynthia likes to use the Silent Treatment if she feels that she has been wronged by you. If you have displeased her, refused a request, or crossed her in any way, she will shut you out by saying nothing to you—not an e-mail, not a nod, not a hello. She creates an impenetrable stone wall that only she can break down to allow communication when she deigns to speak to you. You may wait days or weeks or even longer. She feels that her power is in her resistance, coldness, and stoicism. This is passive-aggressive behavior and calling a process shot on Cynthia—in person, in an e-mail, or a letter—can be a very effective tactic. Also, if it gets worse, you need to *cc* it to your boss or the HR department and ask them to intervene.

Explanation

People like Cynthia are maddening to deal with. She has a sadistic streak and she feels powerless about her rage and anger, so she resorts to this vindictive passive-aggressive level because she knows it's effective, hurtful, and upsetting, and it will drive people crazy. She won't communicate because she doesn't want to lose, and in her mind, communication would put her on an even playing field with her opponent, where she has to be accountable. Communication in an office setting demands that its participants be mature, reasonable, and logical. Cynthia probably doesn't consider herself as being immature, unreasonable, or illogical, but she still feels that she's justified in acting this way because she knows it will drive you nuts. Calling process is a good thing to do with Cynthia so she is confronted on her childish behavior; at least she will know you're on to her game and that you won't be sucked into it. She can be a negative vortex, so avoid being drawn into her immature maneuvers.

Solution

Cynthia, I think we should have a talk. I really enjoy working with you because you're good at your job and you always have an interesting angle from which to take on projects. However, I can't help notice that sometimes there seems to be a communication barrier between us. Speak up and correct me if I'm wrong, but I feel like you're giving me the silent treatment right now to punish me, and I would like to know what I did to warrant this. It seems like an immature power play on your part, and I know that you've done this to me before and to others. Let's have a conversation about this instead of your not talking to me, and I'm sure we'll get this matter sorted out in no time. I hope so, because as I said, I really do enjoy working with you. So tell me, what are you angry about? What can I do to remedy the situation here?

The Sugarcoater

Situation

Susie the Sugarcoater hates being direct, confrontational, or blunt when she has something nasty to say, so she sugarcoats everything she says and does with sweetness, smiles, kindness, and pleasantries. Don't be fooled by the façade. Sugarcoaters feel that social graces are the most important thing in the world, and they sacrifice the truth to be sweet, acceptable, and pleasant. You know in your gut that things are not right, and it is maddening to deal with a sugarcoater because you usually never get a straight answer. Honesty may be too painful for them and sugarcoaters sometimes live in their own little bubble. That doesn't work in the real world of business.

Explanation

Susie was probably raised by a mother who told her that being direct was impolite and taught her how to get her way by sugarcoating everything. Susie is afraid of bluntness, honesty, and the hard truth because it's too painful for her to accept the harsh realties of life. Susie can be fragile or she may be a "steel magnolia"—very strong, tenacious, and determined beneath a polite, soft exterior. Sometimes she lives in an imaginary world and has to pretend that things are better than they seem. If she's the person to bring you bad news about the sales figures, finances, or the stock price, you're not going to get an accurate picture. Her rose-colored glasses can misinterpret whatever data they come across, if the data doesn't conform to her vision of the world. Susie is definitely not the person for a job that deals in harsh realities. Her tact and diplomacy are better served as an event planner for the company, greeting visiting executives and their families and arranging niceties for the firm, where her lovely social skills can be utilized. If you find that Susie is the "wrong tool for the job," perhaps you can mention this to her boss and to HR and she can be transferred to a more appropriate position for her talents.

Solution

Susie, I appreciate your pleasantness and sweetness around the office. It's really easy to have a conversation with you. Sometimes, however, I find that you perhaps put too positive a spin on things and avoid any trace of negativity. I'd much rather have you give it to me straight than sugarcoat things. If we know exactly what shape we're in, no matter how bad it may be, then we can figure out how to deal with it and reverse that condition. If we think everything is fine when it's not, then we risk being caught unaware or in a precarious position. So please tell me the bad news about things along with the good, because I'd really like to continue working cooperatively with you, OK? Thanks!

The Smiling Cobra

Situation

Sander the Smiling Cobra is a power monger who smiles while he stabs you in the back. He is usually climbing the ladder of success and thinks that by destroying his competition, he'll be on the fast track. Sander's smiling face belies the treacherous nature of a smiling cobra. He's like Susie the Sugarcoater, but he knows reality and deals with the truth. He is just a phony manipulator and you know it. He will use people to get what he needs and will step on anyone to get there. You feel he is using you and you've caught him in various lies, even trying to set you up to take the fall. You sense he's dangerous and that you need to get away from him as quickly as possible.

Explanation

Sander learned to always keep up appearances, to never tell anyone how he really feels, and to fake his way through life, staying true only to his hidden agenda of ambition, ruthlessness, greed, and power. He usually has no inner moral compass, no conscience, is a pathological liar, and convinces himself he's right. He usually doesn't feel any guilt and has no empathy or compassion but will fake it, as a good actor will. He sets you up, then sabotages your plans, suggestions, or results, and blames you to take the fall. Sander is envious of others' success and has to make others wrong and look bad. His guile, good looks, charm, natural intelligence, and street smarts have gotten him far in life as he's climbed the ladder, but if you look closely, it's strewn with people he's stepped on to get there. He is usually a manipulative individual and is not to be trusted. He can be charming one minute and viciously intimidating the next. He can be very dangerous and will throw you under the bus in a nanosecond to get what he wants. He can usually be described as a sociopathic, psychopathic or antisocial personality. When you confront him, he'll most likely not change, but at least he'll be on notice that you're aware of his tricks. He may also resent it and take out his revenge on you. So save up your proof and documentation and take it to your boss and to HR, because you're going to need bigger guns when you deal with him. Remember, he's devious, ruthlessly ambitious, and a backstabber, smiling all the while. These individuals are capable of anything, including murder. Get away from him as fast as possible. You have every right to refuse to work with him.

Solution

Sander, I admire your ambition and know that you have big things planned for yourself. It's how *you get there that concerns me. You've told me certain things and then changed your mind. You've promised me things and then I come to find out that they're never going to happen. It's one thing when circumstances change, cutbacks happen, and we all have to accommodate. It's another thing when you distort the truth or tell lies of omission and attempt to sabotage me. I'd rather have you be up-front about things and be honest than twist or withhold the facts, because when you do that, my trust level in you drops and I waste time second-guessing you. So I have found that you're not trustworthy. I'm on to your game, and you and your lies have been discovered to be false.*

The Thief

Situation

Thane the Thief steals objects from your desk, your purse, or the back of your chair. He can take anything—your precious mementos, cash, supplies, clothes, or food. Perhaps you haven't seen him do it; perhaps other co-workers have seen him take things in the past. Either way, you know that your things are missing and you suspect Thane. He may take possessions that seemingly have no meaning for him; it might just be a way to get back at you.

Explanation

Thane may be a compulsive thief or his stealing could be part of an unconscious effort to "belong" or to join an interoffice group, as strange as that may sound. Thieves feel out of the loop and want to be "in." Of course, there's always the kleptomaniac who does it as a pathological habit that he or she can't break. Some do it to get revenge, to be mean-spirited, and to hurt you by taking what's yours. Whatever the motivation, Thane definitely needs professional help, and if you know for sure that it was he who stole your items, you need to tell him so. Reporting him to HR is important too, but be sure you have proof first to substantiate your case.

If you don't know for sure who the person was who stole from you, you can make a general report to HR, listing the items, the time you knew they were missing, and other details. The next best thing to do is to lock away your valuable stuff in the office, your desk drawer, or a locker for the near future. Keep your purse with you at all times or lock it up, too. When you confront Thane, don't tell him whether you're going to report it to HR or to the police or not. Keep him guessing because he needs the extra pressure of not knowing if the law or HR will be involved. Remember, this behavior may be a cry for help from someone who unconsciously or consciously knows he has a serious problem and is asking someone to report him. Many times, these people will do anything to cover their tracks, so be very careful with them. You may want to go to HR and confront Thane in front of the HR representative. That way you will be covered, and there will be a report filed on him. Use the proper channels in dealing with someone like Thane.

Solution

Thane, I know that you sit over at the end of the row here. The other day, I noticed some things were missing from my desk, and when I passed your cubicle, I saw them under your desk and I'd like them back right now. I don't know what provokes you to take things from me; however, it needs to stop immediately. I can report this to our boss and also to HR. So please return my things to me right now, and don't let it happen again. I hope you know that you can be reported and arrested for theft. I am going to ask that you get some professional help if you want to continue working in this office. Otherwise, I will need to report you to HR and to the police. Here's a list of the psychotherapists who are preferred providers on our insurance plan and here's the phone number and address of our Employee Assistance Program. I hope that you get help.

The Idea and Credit Stealer

Situation

Ivan the Idea Stealer steals your ideas and passes them off as his own or he takes credit for work you've done. People like Ivan usually don't unconsciously absorb something you've said and mistakenly assert it as their own idea; rather, they blatantly take an idea of yours and put it forth as their own when you are not around. It could be your ideas about expanding a better marketing plan, a new ad campaign, or the latest statistics for the report. It's important to stop him, though, so that your ideas can remain *your* ideas and you get the credit you deserve for further promotions, raises, and awards.

Explanation

Ivan is usually unethical, selfish, and sneaky. He may be tapping into your computer, going through your desk when you leave, or peeping over your shoulder. He is smart but too lazy to come up with anything original, so instead he takes the easy way out by stealing your ideas and taking credit for your work. If you suspect you have an Ivan in your office, you *must* protect yourself from him. Change your password daily. Shut down and lock your computer and take your purse with you at lunch as well as during coffee and bathroom breaks. Put important data on a thumb drive and keep it with you so he can't break into your computer. Taking these measures will help deter him in the future; however, it's also important to confront Ivan directly about what he's done because he may think you don't know. Let him know that you won't stand for it. Send your ideas to your boss as quickly as you come up with them so you can protect your innovations without Ivan stealing them. You may want to send yourself the ideas as a certified return-receipt-requested letter, so you have a date or time stamp when they were created. If you have more lucrative ideas that need intellectual property protection, then find an attorney to register them as copyrights, patents, or trademarks as fast as possible. You can also do it yourself online with the government's website and through the mail or courier services. Be prepared for spending time and money either way, but it's worth it.

Solution

Ivan, we have to work together and I'd like that to be as pleasant and as cooperative as possible. I've noticed that several times you've had some ideas that were so similar to mine, it couldn't possibly have been by coincidence. You did it in the meeting yesterday and I was shocked. I believe that you took the ideas from me by looking at my notes or my computer, or you overheard me running them by Jill. I think it would be best for everyone that you admit to our supervisor that the idea you proposed was really mine and relinquish the credit. I'm sure you'll be forgiven and then you'll have the chance to prove the strength of your own ideas next time. If there's a next time with you taking my ideas and passing them off as your own, though, the consequences will be dire. I will go to HR and get an attorney if I have to. Do I make myself clear? Stop stealing my ideas!

The Naysayer

Situation

Nadine the Naysayer is like Rachel Dratch's character Debbie Downer on "Saturday Night Live." She will tell you a million reasons why your idea will never work, without adding any constructive feedback. She's a wet blanket, a spoiler, and a doomsday predictor. Her pessimism is toxic and poisons the air around everyone. Even when things are going well, she will say something negative to bring the mood down. Nothing ever seems to be right in her eyes, and she can never seem to find the silver lining in a rain cloud. It can be so depressing to work with her after a while. Perhaps down deep, Nadine doesn't want others to succeed and may say or do something negative to spoil it when they do.

Explanation

Nadine may be afraid of success herself and her whole life seems to be motivated by fear. Perhaps her parents were overly cautious, negative, and overprotective, so Nadine absorbed their fear and never developed courage, faith, and the ability to cope with life's travails. No matter—you have to set limits with her and get her to stop her doom-and-gloom diatribes around you and others. Nadine has probably been disappointed many times in her life and has learned not to trust happiness, success, or optimistic outlooks. Her expectations have not been met so she is envious of others' success. Nadine has developed a pessimistic attitude about most things, and she is frightened to take a risk herself. She views the world as a very dangerous, unsafe place, full of pitfalls, horrors, and disappointments. What Nadine doesn't seem to realize is that her thoughts act like steamrollers paving the way for her actions or her fate. She is setting herself up for failure by her negative thinking. She calls herself a "realist," while many people would call her a pessimist. Nadine needs to do the "Best Scenario to Worst Scenario" exercise. There's a difference between preparing yourself for the worst and thinking that the worst is always going to happen. Nadine revels in "I told you so," and she loves it when things go wrong because it confirms her view of the world as a hostile, negative place full of toxic, cruel, and powerful people who thwart her every hope and move. It confirms her view of herself as a powerless victim at the hands of powerful, uncaring forces. Nadine is afraid to hope, to think positively, and to act in a bold manner to achieve her dreams and goals. What she also misses is that setbacks are part of life—they are the hurdles we all have to jump to achieve our dreams. You just jump over them, go around them, wiggle under them, or weave through them. That's how we learn, get strong, and make our goals come true. You can't let negative people like Nadine get in your way when you're striving for a creative breakthrough, so protect yourself from her and set boundaries. Avoid her when possible.

Solution

Nadine, I appreciate how you can see all the pitfalls in our proposed solutions. It's healthy during a project to take a pragmatic, realistic look at things, rather than going on blind optimism. That's an important evaluation skill you have, especially in research, design, and development, and I welcome your analyses about projects. If you focused your observations toward finding something positive to say during these brainstorming sessions, however, it would be much more productive. When we have to work together, please give me your feedback without the negativity; or, if you have something negative to say, back it up with facts about why you think it won't work or tell me how to make it better. I would appreciate it because I'd like to work well with you. Thanks.

The Envious One

Situation

Enid the Envious One never feels she has enough. When she looks at other people, her eyes and brain operate like cash registers, totaling up their salaries and the amount of money they must spend on clothes, shoes, purses, suits, and haircuts. Everything seems to be a comparison with Enid, and things are always coming up short on her end. The way she vents her displeasure at this injustice is by griping about it to whoever will listen (usually you) and trying to thwart others. She can also be a gossip and turn people against you because of her envy.

Explanation

Enid feels insecure about what she has versus what she should have. She feels inadequate and angry, has low self-esteem, and bases her identity on material possessions—or her lack of them. She usually talks about other people in superficial and material terms because that's all she sees. Perhaps she grew up on the wrong side of the tracks in an affluent community or was a scholarship student at a private school. She probably always felt "one down" and never had the money to compete with the wealthy kids at school. She still has a chip on her shoulder to this day. She may even have come from an affluent family and still feels it's never enough. Her venomous remarks are vicious and she can go after you or people she is envious of by spreading rumors, sabotaging them, stealing their ideas, and a myriad of other tactics. Enid is probably a narcissistic personality who really has difficulty forming genuine relationships and friendships because of her preoccupation with superficial, materialistic, and shallow concerns. Be very wary of Enid!

Solution

Enid, I like the work you turn in, and you always pull your weight at our meetings. I find, however, that your conversations about other people are interfering with my productivity. I'm really not concerned with what salaries people earn, what designer clothes they wear, or what car they drive. I have a job to do and I need to concentrate on that and I'd like you to do the same.

I would appreciate talking about the job, rather than your suspicions about which of our co-workers makes more money and whether they deserve it or what trips they took. I hope we can work together because I think we'd get along just fine if not for that. I hope you understand that my focus and your focus is on our job here and we need to concentrate on that.

The Practical Joker

Situation

Perry the Practical Joker puts whoopee cushions on your seat, has buzzers in his palm when he shakes your hand, and places rubber vomit near or on your desk because he thinks all of this is funny. You must tell him that it's not—in fact, it wastes time, distracts people from doing their work, and can embarrass people and hurt their feelings. Someone could even go into cardiac arrest at the shock of some of Perry's practical "jokes." Everyone likes a joke now and then, but Perry goes too far and doesn't know when to be serious.

Explanation

As a kid, Perry probably was the "class clown" and got a lot of attention making people laugh. He may also have loved the attention of getting yelled at for putting plastic dog poop on the rug to upset his mother. If Perry's parents were stoic, uptight, rigid, and uncommunicative, getting negative attention was better than getting no attention at all for Perry. At least he was getting a reaction from them. That is usually what motivates the practical joker. He also likes to see people make fools of themselves, especially if it's his revenge for being taunted and made fun of as a child or for how you embarrassed him at the office (whether inadvertently or not). He is turning the tables on what was done to him to get revenge. He may be a seething cauldron of rage underneath the practical joker veneer. But enough is enough, and Perry needs to have some limits set for himself.

Solution

Perry, many people share your wacky sense of humor and enjoy your practical jokes, and some of it is funny. Other people, and I include myself in this group, think it is infantile and would only find it funny if this was the fifth grade. This is an office and you're distracting people. They're getting angry at you, but they won't say anything. Please stop playing pranks on your co-workers and on me. Many of your practical jokes are inappropriate and hurtful. I would hate to have to report it to our boss or HR, because I'd rather not see you get written up or even fired, but if this keeps up I will. I hope you will heed my warning and keep the joking out of the office. Why don't you write your own stand-up routine and do it at open mike night at some comedy clubs? That might be a good venue for your humor, and you might even land your own sitcom if you were funny enough. I hope you understand how I feel and how others feel here. I hope you change. I wish you well in your comedy career.

CHAPTER 30

The Politicians

The Political Soap Boxer
The Office Politician
The Brownnoser
The Ladder Climber
The Boss's Relative

Whether it's in the halls of Congress, the White House, or a small business in Des Moines, Iowa, every workplace hosts an undercurrent of political activity at all times. It can change in an instant depending on a new boss being appointed, people being downsized, companies merging or going bankrupt, and a host of other factors. Office politics is about power—who has it, who doesn't have it, and who wants to get it. How people go about getting it is what office politics are about—are your colleagues ethical, up-front, and hard-working in their efforts? Or are they devious, backstabbing, and vicious? Power, like money, is neutral; it's *how* you use it that makes the difference. So watch and listen for the power dynamics at your workplace before you say anything or make any comments about someone because it can change in an instant. Office politics are a fact of life. Here are the various types you may find in the workplace.

The Political Soap Boxer

Situation

Porter the Political Soap Boxer uses every opportunity to rail against the political forces that he feels are thwarting his existence, his paycheck, and his rights. He can be a Republican, Democrat, Independent, Socialist, Communist, or Libertarian—it doesn't matter. He will stand by the watercooler, send e-mails, or catch you in an elevator to expound on what he thinks you should know. He may be an idealogue looking for recruits to his political party, or he may just want to vent. He seldom asks your opinion but harangues you with his diatribe quite frequently, wherever you may be. Whether you agree with him or not, you're tired of it and want it to stop.

Explanation

Porter is passionate about politics and he really should be working actively for his chosen political party promoting its agenda, where he would be much happier and probably feel more productive. Most of the time, the Porters of the world don't see the other side of an issue, are not open to discussion or debate, and feel "it's my way or the highway." They can be pushy, insensitive, and close-minded. People like Porter are not usually good listeners, and they often fail to acknowledge another's viewpoint. They can be adamant, inflexible, boorish bullies, so be careful. You still have to set limits because you have a right not to hear the rants.

Solution

Porter, I admire your passion for politics and how you care about public policy, the government, and the system. It does feel inappropriate at times to be getting an earful about some of the things you discuss here at the office, walking into the building, or in the elevator. I really hope that you can restrict your political discussions and opinions to yourself and after hours because I have work to do and I don't want to engage in any political debates or discussions while I'm at work and on the clock. If I want to discuss politics with you, I'll approach you. I have to concentrate on what I have at hand and I would also not care to have certain opinions of mine known throughout the office. I appreciate it because you're a good worker and I enjoy being on projects with you. I hope we can continue to work together with these new parameters. Thanks!

The Office Politician

Situation

There are ethical, caring, upstanding politicians, I'm sure. Patrick the Office Politician is similar to the worst stereotypes of politicians everywhere—he knows how to maneuver to reach his goals, and he has a nose for where the power is and is not. He knows how to get ahead, what to say to whom and when. He knows how to be subtle, tactful, and diplomatic, as well as how to intimidate, play hardball when he has to, and circumvent people's authority. He can talk out of both sides of his mouth, betray people, play two opposing sides against each other, plant seeds of doubt, and set people up to fail. He can gather data on people and use it against them for his own gain as blackmail. You don't trust him and rightly so.

Explanation

Politicians are notorious for keeping their own interests above everything else—their goal is to maintain power and get reelected. Office politicians are similarly focused on keeping their job, getting promoted, and rising through the ranks, so their tactics and goals overlap. People like Patrick will use you to get ahead, and they will stab you in the back if you cross them. They don't connect their behavior to consequences and are all about getting what they need *now.* They worry about the effects and consequences later. They are slick and manipulative. They feel they can talk their way out of any situation because they think they're smarter and more clever than you. They have a history of negative and unethical behavior—in relationships, with spouses or partners, with money management, and in business. Be very wary of them. They can and usually will throw you under a bus if you get in their way.

Solution

Patrick, I admire your ambition and your commitment to success. Sometimes I feel that you step over the line and put me and others in untenable posi-

tions. I don't want to be put in situations where you're asking me to do things that I feel are unethical. You have a manner of talking your way in or out of anything around here, but I can see right through you, and you're not going to get off that easily with me. I refuse to go along with your schemes so please know that. Tell me what you want up front without any hidden agendas and I'll see if I can agree to it. If I can, then we can work together, and if I can't and don't, I won't. Please send me e-mails about what you need and want and when. I'll read them and judge it accordingly Thanks.

The Brownnoser

Situation

Ben the Brownnoser always flatters the higher-ups, seeking praise, acknowledgment, and advancement. Mostly, though, Ben has his sights set on a promotion, a raise, and eventually his nameplate on the desk in a corner office. He has high aspirations and uses people to get ahead. Many times, Ben just uses flattery to "win friends and influence people." He takes the Dale Carnegie Course to heart, but without the heart—he's superficial and lacks sincerity and conviction. His false flattery will be sprinkled on you if he thinks you can get him somewhere other than his cubicle. Sometimes he flatters only those he thinks can advance his cause, and other times he flatters everyone around him, just in case. Be wary you don't get the Bens!

Explanation

Ben is ambitious and wants promotions, raises, and perhaps to even run the company. He thinks he can achieve that by flattery, being a "yes-man," and getting people to like him. People like Ben usually don't have a strong spine, so they align themselves with the powers that be. Ben will never outwardly say a bad thing about someone because he knows to never burn a bridge. Other times, the flattery is to prevent you from being mean to him, confronting him, or holding him accountable. He puts on a front of being "Mr. Nice Guy" and uses it as a defense mechanism to protect himself. Unfortunately for Ben, he doesn't realize that since he comes off sounding insincere and phony, most people don't trust him because they sense he would throw them under the bus to get ahead. Trust your intuition on that.

Solution

Ben, I thank you for your compliments. When you mean them, I appreciate them. There are times I feel that the compliments aren't really sincere—that you are saying them to get something from me or because you want to make up for a mistake you made. I'd much rather have you be direct and honest with me about what you want than try to butter me up to get on my good side. I would feel more comfortable that way. You don't have to flatter me. So please, tell me what you need and I'll be happy to see if I can help you or not. I hope to be able to work cooperatively with you.

The Ladder Climber

Situation

Lenny the Ladder Climber is like Ben the Brownnoser in his ambitions. He is also like Patrick the Office Politician, but without the tact and diplomacy. Lenny the Ladder Climber may or may not be all that ruthless or cruel. Lenny can be totally oblivious to anyone else's efforts in his relentless pursuit of getting ahead, or he can be deliberate, vicious, and Machiavellian, as he plots his way to the corner office. Lenny will use you and anyone else to achieve his goals.

Explanation

Feeling insecure, usually suffering from a case of advanced and chronic greed, Lenny believes that money, power, and status will ultimately make him happy. People like Lenny can be sharks, con men, rip-off artists, and they do it all under the guise of bettering the company. Calling a process shot is the best and most effective way to deal with this type. You must protect yourself in every way from the Lennys of the world. *Snakes in Suits: When Psychopaths Go to Work*, by Paul Babiak and Robert D. Hare, is an excellent book to read about the Lennys of the world. Be wary!

Solution

Lenny, I appreciate your ambition and the way you follow your goals. I've noticed that you sometimes twist my words into what you want to hear, instead of what I actually said. I feel that you use me and other people to get what you want. We all want to get ahead, Lenny, but there's a right way to do things and a wrong way. In the future I'd like you to tell me honestly and directly what you want instead of manipulating me. I'm watching you because, frankly, I don't trust you. We can work together if you play by the rules and cut the phony act and your manipulation. So I hope you'll honor what I'm saying to you.

The Boss's Relative

Situation

Bobby the Boss's Relative knows he's going to get preferential treatment and get away with things that other employees could never do. There are some Bobbys of the world who choose differently—they work hard to make sure they prove themselves the equal of any other employee despite being the boss's son or relative. Unfortunately, in many cases, it's the former. Bobby often comes in late, leaves early, delegates as much work as he can, and outright dumps some of it on you. If and when you confront Bobby, you must prepare yourself for being reprimanded. If it's a family business, most times Bobby will be kept in the company despite wrongdoings, proof of misdeeds, and incompetence.

Explanation

"Blood is thicker than water" certainly applies here. Loyalty, guilt, duty, and responsibility keep incompetent relatives in a family business, so many times you just have to learn patience, tolerance, and smart coping mechanisms to deal with Bobby. He knows he'll never get fired, and for years he has gotten away with much undisciplined and, yes, toxic behavior. However, if he's personally giving you a lot of grief, it's your responsibility to let him know you will not stand for it. You must document everything with e-mails, letters, and proof of his wrongdoings, or you will be powerless to make your point. You can go to HR, who might or might not be a relative. HR may also feel its hands are tied in a family business and can do nothing to protect workers. Be prepared for the possibility of getting fired, however, if you confront the boss or even go to HR. That may be the sad reality in some family-owned businesses.

Solution

Bobby, I realize that you're the boss's nephew, and I understand you think that he probably won't ever reprimand you. The reality is you work for the company, and the operative word here is work. *Like any CEO, your uncle knows financial risks when he sees them. And he'd be quite upset if he knew that your behavior had been disturbing the balance of this office and getting in the way of people like me increasing his profits. I want you to know I'm not going to do your work for you any longer, nor will I cover for you when you are late, so please don't ask me. I need to concentrate on finishing my assignments and I hope you do the same. I really wish that you'd develop commitment and dedication for work that you really love or find another job or career that you love. You may feel that you have to work here because it's the family business and maybe you like it and maybe you don't. However you feel, do the best you can at whatever job you have—whether it's here or somewhere else—and prove to yourself that you can do it and that you're not here just because of nepotism.*

CHAPTER 31

The Sexually Suggestive

The Seducer/The Seductress

The Flatterer

The Flirt

The Sexual Harasser

The Office Couple

The Office Affair

The Jealous One/The Stalker

The Mistress

The Boy Toy

The Sexually Suggestive types have similar tactics, aims, and goals as the Politicians, including manipulation, bribery, and flattery, with the added factor of using sex, or at least the promise of sex, to get ahead or get their way. Sex is a tool or a skill, like typing, that they feel able to use to their benefit. They are willing to compromise their morals (if they have any) when it comes to giving or demanding sexual favors to achieve their ends.

Young women who are ethical and honest, yet financially strapped, needing the job and the benefits, can fall prey to the office predators. Seductive women looking to sleep their way to the top demean other hardworking, honest women by using sex to get ahead. Lecherous co-workers and those with inappropriate boundaries get sexually involved with others at work and use employees because of their own sexual demands. This can cause arguments because of jealousy and suspicion. It is very poisonous to a company.

Keep sex out of the workplace. If you fall in love with someone at work, take a lateral move to another department within the company or find another job, but do not get involved with people you work with. It's too dangerous for your reputation, for the company, and for your partner. Some people have been accused of sexual harassment when they were just giving someone a genuine, nonsexual compliment that was taken the wrong way, and you don't want that on your record or in your personnel file. There will always be suspicion, even if you're cleared. People in the Sexually Suggestive group can be very sneaky and manipulative—if they're caught, they can try to set you up to take the blame—so document everything.

The Seducer/The Seductress

Situation

Selena the Seductress and Sheldon the Seducer are after one thing—your body and then ultimately favors—a raise, a promotion, or the corner office. Whether it's a man or a woman as the target, the seducer/seductress uses the same tactics—flattery, sexual flirtation, teasing, luring, and the promise of great sex, whether they intend to deliver it or not. It's all about getting what they want: a long-term affair, company secrets, or another notch on their belt or lipstick case, as Pat Benatar sang. Sheldon might "accidentally" rub up against you or brush his hand by "mistake" against your breast or buttocks. Selena might wear revealing outfits around the office in an effort to entice you, or they both might come at you in a more low-key way by occasionally whispering in your ear or presenting you with gifts. One way or the other, though, when you are the target of someone else's sexual conquest, you will know it! And after the sexual "affair" is over and they have gotten what they were after, they will usually dump you. So be prepared to not get enticed into their lethal web in the first place.

Explanation

Sheldon and Selena both want something from you—your secret pass code, confidential information, or possibly even a green card. Whatever they want, it's not to be your friend, lover, or spouse, even though they'll make you think it is. It's about them getting what they want. Even if they're genuinely interested in you, sincere people who want a healthy, happy relationship don't start it off with seductive, sexy moves in an office setting. They may flirt with you, try to catch your eye, and chat you up, but they genuinely want to get to know you as a person and they aim to develop a solid friendship first. So be very wary of someone who appears to be trying to seduce you! They are not to be trusted.

Solution

Selena/Sheldon, the attention is a bit much. I have work to do here and I feel you're constantly coming on to me when I'm just not interested. Please stop the flirtations because it's very inappropriate. If there's something you want from me, just ask and I'll see if I can help you with it, but you're not winning any points with me this way. I just want to keep business separated from my personal life. I'm sure you can understand that. So what do you really want? Tell me directly and then I can decide. Stop the games and be honest and direct with me. Thanks.

The Flatterer

Situation

Frannie the Flatterer knows how to be subtle, but she will also look you straight in the eye and shower you with flirtatious compliments. She can use clever psychological techniques to tell you what you love to hear—how smart, witty, powerful, and charismatic you are. It's the siren call, and she'll mesmerize you in an instant. Frannie is similar to Ben the Brownnoser and to Selena/Sheldon the Seducer. She can use the flattery to bank favors around the office or even for the victory of getting you into bed. Frannie may or may not want sex, but she's smoother and more subtle than Sheldon and Selena, and maybe even more dangerous.

Explanation

People like Frannie have been conditioned since childhood to use compliments to get their way and win you over. Sometimes it sounds sincere, but other times, it smacks of manipulation and insincerity. They may just be innocuously flattering you as a force of habit, but they also may have hidden agendas. Frannie is like Ben the Brown-noser except that instead of focusing on the higher-ups, she is more likely to target her co-workers. She believes her compliments are accruing interest in her "bank account" with you, so when she wants to make "a withdrawal" and get information or a favor, she thinks you owe her and she's entitled to it. Wrong! You must set Frannie straight.

Solution

Frannie, your genuine compliments are kind and well meaning, and I appreciate them. I find, though, that your compliments can tend toward flattery and insincerity. I can't help noticing that it seems that you really pour them on when you want something—a favor, an exception to a rule, or to get out of work—and I see through it. I'm not willing to do your work for you anymore. I'd much rather have you cut the phony flattery and tell me what you want. Please be direct and honest with me. It's just a better way of interacting. I'm happy to do you a favor if I can, and if I think it's unreasonable, then I'll tell you. OK? Thanks!

The Flirt

Situation

Flicka the Flirt is a playful tease. She shoots you tantalizing, sexy looks, showers you with compliments, and brings you little gifts. She conveys the promise of sexual interest, but the question is, "To what end?" You must ask yourself, "What does she really want?" At first, you think she is interested in you, but as you observe her behavior in the office, you may see that she does this to other people as well, so you doubt her sincerity. You're tired of the come-on because you know it's not genuine and she wants something else. Maybe she offers sex and maybe she doesn't; either way, it is manipulative, deceitful, and lethal. You simply don't trust her and you shouldn't!

Explanation

Flicka wants something and it's for her to know and you to find out. She probably learned how to get what she wanted from her parents by being "cute" and sweet-natured. Her mother or father gave in immediately each time, and so the personality of a flirt was born. You have to call a process shot on the flirts; otherwise, they'll keep doing it. They'll set you up and you'll be so flattered, mesmerized, and addicted to their slick routine that you won't even know when you're giving in to their hidden agenda and getting them what they want. Be wary of the flirts.

Flickas usually have a plan, and you may be the sap who will be taken for a ride, like how Kathleen Turner manipulated William Hurt in *Body Heat*. Let's make a distinction between the insincere flirts and the people who are genuinely interested in you, trying to get your attention so you'll ask them out or so they feel they have a chance to ask you out. You can tell by the person's demeanor when someone legitimately likes you and wants you to like him or her back; in terms of office romances, those are the keepers. The insincere flirts are not. Just be careful of the pitfalls of office romances and possibly being accused of sexual harassment. Get to know someone first. Don't become sexually involved. Work on the friendship. And if one develops, then you will have to deal with the dilemma of having an office romance, which I don't recommend. As the expression goes, "Don't get your honey where you get your money."

Solution

Flicka, your compliments are quite flattering, and I thank you. What I have been noticing, though, is it feels like you're flirting with me to get something that you want. I don't know what that is, and it doesn't matter. What matters is you are not going to get it by flirting with me. So as nice as it might be to get this kind of attention from you, I must ask you to stop it. I'd rather have you simply ask me for whatever it is that you want. So what is it?

The Sexual Harasser

Situation

Sewell the Sexual Harasser may start out with compliments and flirting but he's different from Flicka the Flirt in that he is more blatant about his intentions. He crosses the line from innuendo to outright propositioning and grabbing, rubbing against you, or sneaking kisses when you're unaware. When you object, sometimes he covers it by saying, "Oh, I was just kidding," or "You're too sensitive," or "Can't you take a joke?" Sometimes he will say, "You were coming on to me and you know it! Stop being such a tease. You know you were asking for this! So stop playing the innocent virgin!" There is nothing funny about sexual harassment, though, and that's exactly what this behavior is.

Explanation

Sewell usually can't take a hint that you're not interested. People like him need to be confronted directly about their illegal behavior, reported to HR, and perhaps even sued, if they've made you feel cheap or exploited. Sometimes that is the only wake-up call they will respond to. In instances of outright harassment, you need not start out on a positive note or use the "Sandwich" because Sewell may feel that is a sign of weakness in you, that his behavior is acceptable, and that you like what he's doing. Just be blunt, direct, and confrontational. Whether you go immediately to HR or give a warning is up to you, and it depends on the severity of the harassment. Document everything you can. If you have any witnesses who are willing to step forward and go to HR with you, by all means bring them along.

Solution

Sewell, what you are doing is considered sexual harassment, and I resent it. This is illegal and I'm going to report it to HR. You can't rub up against me, grab me, or make suggestive remarks about my body. What makes you think you can get away with that kind of obnoxious behavior? The things you've said to me could not only get you fired, they could get you sued. And I just may do that. So stop it now!

The Office Couple

Situation

Otto and Orinda are the office couple—they are love puppies. They are hot for each other—whether they're dating, just flirting, or married. And they can't help but remind you of how hot they are for each other at every available, inappropriate moment. Several scenarios can involve you and the workplace with the Office Couple:

- They drag co-workers into their fights to take sides and you resent it and their drama.
- They circle the wagons and tightly close out co-workers from their intimate little world for two.
- They engage in public displays of affection in the lunchroom, in the breakroom, or in front of others, and some people think it's inappropriate and feel uneasy, embarrassed, and even envious. You want to tell them, "Get a room!"
- If they've had a fight the previous night, it feels like a cold war in the workplace.
- If they're in a honeymoon period, they're lovey-dovey, distracting others, and may not be getting their work done.

Whatever the scenario, the Office Couple can't separate work from their personal life. Many businesses have strict policies against anyone dating, married, or divorced working for the same company. There are many logical business reasons for enforcing this rule, since it can and does affect the work environment and ultimately productivity and the bottom line. Know what your company's policies are on this topic in case this happens in your office or even if it happens to you. It's simply inappropriate.

Explanation

Otto and Orinda may have difficulties with boundary issues—they shouldn't be mixing their personal lives up in a work environment, but they do. This may be their first love or they may be divorced and on the rebound, or they may be widowed and never thought they'd find anyone again. They may be especially codependent and not know how to set limits with each other. They may also not realize how disruptive their coupling is for the rest of the people at the office, and they need to be told directly before they get into trouble with the higher-ups. It's unprofessional for them to bring their personal relationship into the office, and they need to get that message, one way or the other. Be tactful, firm, and discreet. Confront them together and in private, perhaps away from the office.

Solution

Otto and Orinda, I know you're in love [or happily married] and want to be together all the time. It's wonderful to have a close relationship [marriage] like you two have. However, it's also very distracting for me and for others here at the office because of your interactions. Your public displays of affection are inappropriate and need to stop. When you have a spat, you need to leave it out of the office. Asking me and others to take sides during an argument is simply not fair. It's divisive in an office setting and it must stop. If you can't do this, you might want to think of working in different departments and just having lunch together. I feel awkward talking to you about this, but I felt that I had to say something because I like you both and I don't want to see you disciplined for something that you could just stop or do later in the day or in the evening. Thanks so much for hearing me out. I hope you make appropriate changes to your relationship here at the office, because I enjoy working with both of you.

The Office Affair

Situation

Oscar and Olivia are having an affair. They both may be married to other people, or maybe only one of them is married, but either way, they're trying to hide their adulterous behavior and they're not doing a very good job of it. The problems of the Office Couple of Otto and Orinda can be the same ones with the Office Affair of Oscar and Olivia. Both situations can be awkward and embarrassing for co-workers to have to deal with. However, the Office Affair has another dimension to it that may compromise your ethical values. If one or both are married to someone else, you may get stuck covering for them when their spouse or partner calls on the telephone. They may ask you to cover for them when they sneak off to a hotel for an extended lunch hour or an out-of-town business trip. They may take off on a Friday and ask you to tell the boss that they're working from home. You just don't want to get involved, and rightfully so. You have a right to speak up and to say that you refuse to continue in their ruse.

Explanation

Oscar and Olivia may be bored or lonely in their marriages, they may be looking for excitement, or they may be having an affair as revenge on their spouses whether they're still living together, divorced, or separated. Regardless of how you feel about their lack of ethics, they are roping you in to cover for them, protect them, even lie for them, and you resent it. You have every right to not want to play that game and you need to stand up and say so. You may want to say that you know they're having an affair or you may not. If they have told you, then you're in on their little secret. If they haven't told you, you should probably remain silent about their affair or risk becoming complicit. Either way, you still have the right to say that you're not going to cover for them or do their work when they're away from the office without specifically mentioning the affair. If you know about their affair, you can say something like the following:

Solution

Olivia and Oscar, I resent having to cover for you when you take long lunches or lie to your spouses when they call on the phone, so I want you to know I'm not willing to be put in that position any longer. You're going to have to face it yourself if your spouse calls or comes to the office wondering where you are. I don't want to be involved in your deception. I'm not one to pass judgment on anybody, so please know that it has nothing to do with that. I just don't want to be a part of anyone else's drama, or the fallout from it.

The Jealous One/The Stalker

Situation

Jerry the Jealous One has either broken up with or been dumped by someone at work and it's eating him alive with pain, jealousy, and envy. He may talk endlessly about the breakup, pump you for information, or even ask you to spy on his former partner. It is interfering with your work and you resent it. You have to tell Jerry to take his issues elsewhere—to seek counseling, for example.

Explanation

Jerry may be going through normal breakup angst, but it's spilling over on you, distracting you, and interfering with your productivity. If this situation has been going on for a long time, then Jerry should be in individual counseling and a support group to get through this difficult time and to prevent him from taking any regrettable action toward his ex. You might want to gently recommend counseling and hope that he gets the professional help he needs.

Solution

Jerry, I understand you're upset about your breakup. I've been there myself and I know it's painful and you feel rejected. I have to put my foot down, though. I'm not going to spy for you or give you information about your ex. I have work to do and your constant calls are interfering with my productivity. I'm not a professional counselor and I don't have the time or the right skills to help you through this. Perhaps if you took advantage of the five free sessions of counseling from our Employee Assistance Program or the preferred providers who are licensed counselors on our insurance plan, you could get the support you need. I feel that it is for the best that I'm not involved anymore. I hope you understand. You're a good person. I hope you get over this, and I'm sure you'll find a wonderful, long-lasting relationship with someone who loves you and whom you love.

The Mistress

Situation

Melinda the Mistress expects to be treated in a certain way for being the boss's mistress—she wants privileges, she feels that the rules don't apply to her, and she believes she doesn't have to work that hard because the boss will always make an exception for her by keeping her on the payroll in a cushy, undemanding job. She makes you do her work for her, knowing you are unable to complain to the boss because he's the one Melinda is having the affair with. You feel trapped, angry, resentful, and you may feel your ethics are being compromised if one or both of them are married to other people. If you're the boss's assistant and you have to cover for him, and if you have moral or religious feelings about adultery, you may feel even more disgusted by this behavior.

Explanation

Usually women like Melinda sadly believe that they can't make it any other way than through offering their sexual favors. They have absorbed false values from their mothers, fathers, or the culture they live in and mistakenly think that women need a man to get ahead, that sex is the coin of the realm, and they are prepared to pay it. Since a boss who is having an affair can be unpredictable in his response to those who know about it, tact and diplomacy are the guidelines here. If Melinda isn't doing her work, expecting you to cover for her and do her work for her, then you may need to confront her, and potentially go to HR to explain that it's inconvenient and inappropriate for you to have to do two jobs—yours and hers. It's better not to mention her affair with the boss to HR, whether they know or not. You don't want to embarrass or humiliate her, and there's the off chance that it's not true. So focus on what's wrong with her work—she's missing deadlines, she doesn't check it, it looks like it's done in a hurry, and that you're not paid to do her job, too. Be discreet but clear in setting limits with her either in person or through an e-mail.

Solution

Melinda, I have noticed that you aren't getting your work done on time and sometimes it is several days late. You ask me to do it for you and cover for you, and that's not in my job description. I'm not going to do your work for you. We are a team here and each person has to get his or her job done because we're all dependent on each other. Sometimes it seems as though you think the rules don't apply to you and you can get away with not doing your work. You can't. So please finish what you have to do and hand it in on time. I appreciate it because I like to get along with all of my co-workers.

The Boy Toy

Situation

Barry the Boy Toy is the male version of the mistress. He's probably very happy being used for sex, may be getting a boost in his career from the connection—a promotion, raise, or special favors—and is delighted to go along with the convenient arrangement. When Barry asks you to do his work, cover for him, or do special favors for him, though, things have gone too far. If Barry is the boss's Boy Toy (gay or straight), you feel uncomfortable and you don't want to do it. The good news is that you don't have to. You can stand up and be direct.

Explanation

Sometimes Barry isn't all that bright, and other times, he knows exactly what he's doing and what he's got to trade in the barter. Either way, you've got to be diplomatic and confront him. The same basic protocol as with Melinda the Mistress applies here. If Barry is having an affair with the boss, you can go to HR, but it's best to confront him first yourself and not mention the relationship between Barry and the boss. Be tactful, firm, and discreet. You're not willing to cover for him or do his work for him.

Solution

Barry, I can't help but notice that you are coming in late and taking long lunches, expecting me to cover for you, and that's not in my job description. We are a team here and each person has to get his or her job done because we're all dependent on each other. Sometimes it seems you think the rules don't apply to you and you can get away with not doing your work. You can't. So please finish what you have to do and hand it in on time. I appreciate it because I like to get along with all of my co-workers. I hope you understand.

CHAPTER 32

The Obsessives

The Missionary
The Food Faddist
The Paranoid
The Perfectionist
The Control Freak
The Critic

The Obsessives are characterized by some or all of the following characteristics: their attention to detail, compulsiveness, hoarding, perfectionism, and rigid persistence. They demand others to agree with them, do as they say, and comply with their wishes. They probably had controlling parents who demanded their children accept their belief system without question, and love was probably conditional, based on adherence and compliance to perfection. Obsessives usually have had some sort of trauma in their life. They may also have an addictive personality, which usually is accompanied by a physiology, metabolism, and thought process that is different from others'. People who make up this group are deserving of your sympathy. At the same time, though, you don't have to endure the grief they give you.

The Missionary

Situation

Mabel the Missionary is out to save your soul. It doesn't matter what religion or faith she believes in—she's out to convert you. She will leave you books, DVDs, CDs, pamphlets, amulets, trinkets, and other accoutrements of her faith. She will preach and pummel you into submission. She'll use your lunch hour to pontificate from her pulpit (aka the cubicle next to yours). You're tired of hearing it and you need to ask her to stop.

Explanation

Mabel was probably brought up in a fundamentalist religion that demanded strict adherence to its religious beliefs under the threat of hellfire and brimstone. Conversely, she may have had no religious upbringing and she has converted to a religion that she now believes in wholeheartedly. Mabel's life is ruled by fear—fear of going to hell, of not being perfect, of having natural human urges and flaws, all of which she tries to repress. She believes that if she converts you, she's going to save her own soul as well as yours. You don't have to be subjected to her diatribes, and you need to set limits and boundaries.

Solution

Mabel, I appreciate that your faith means a great deal to you. I have my own set of beliefs, though, and I really prefer not to be disturbed at work or even outside of work hearing about your religion or anyone else's. I thank you for the pamphlets; I'll return them to you until I feel like reading through them, and then if I want to, I'll ask you for them. I need to concentrate on getting my assignments done while I'm here at work and I'd like you to respect that. I'm sure you understand. So if you can refrain from talking to me about it, I'd greatly appreciate it. And I wish you many blessings.

The Food Faddist

Situation

Fred the Food Faddist looks at your lunch and tells you everything that's wrong with what you're eating—vegetables sprayed with pesticides, dairy products that could have salmonella, meat with nitrates, lurking parasites, E. coli, and preservatives lacing your pudding. You want to hurl before you even start eating. While he may be absolutely right, Fred is annoying. You are not at the dietician's and you haven't asked for his advice; plus, he brings it up at the worst possible time—right when you're about to enjoy the food he's so strongly against. Fred may be in great health and look fabulous—no matter what his age—yet you don't want to hear it and you have the right to and should tell him that. Even if you are interested, he needs to tell you after work, give you a book or magazine articles to read, and not discuss it during lunchtime. He may be genuinely concerned with your health and well-being; you need to thank him for his concern and still set limits and boundaries with him.

Explanation

Fred the Food Faddist is on a mission just like Mabel the Missionary and Porter the Political Soap Boxer—except, instead of religion or politics, he tries to convert you to become a vegetarian, a vegan, a macrobiotic eater, or whatever his food doctrine is. It's annoying and the constant proselytizing is bugging you so much that you don't want to eat lunch anywhere near Fred. He needs to be told to stop. If he doesn't, you can report it to HR.

Solution

Fred, I appreciate how committed you are to your health and it has obviously paid off since you're in such good shape and look years younger than you really are. I've learned a lot from you about diet and nutrition. I'd like you to know, though, that you go a little too far sometimes when you try to convert me to your way of thinking about food. Perhaps you should take your energy and write a book. You've got some excellent information; people just aren't in the mood to hear it at work, especially while they are eating. They feel like you're on a soap box and a rant. I really cherish our friendship and for your own good, I recommend that you stop the food preaching at the office and especially in the lunchroom. I don't want to have to report this to HR, so I'd appreciate your understanding and cooperation. Thanks!

The Paranoid

Situation

Patty the Paranoid is convinced that her bosses and co-workers are out to get her. It may be their sexism, or if she's a minority she may be convinced they are racist, against her religion or ethnic background, or any other classification she falls into. She's told you that she feels she's being discriminated against. You don't see it but you feel sorry for her. If her paranoia increases, she will tell you that they're taping her phone calls; tracking her calls, activities, and computer use; and videotaping her with the new security system. She may be correct or she may be totally wrong. If she's wrong, she may exhibit signs of a serious paranoid mental disorder.

Explanation

Patty distrusts almost everyone because she is terrified of being dependent on anyone. Paranoia is a fear of dependency, and to guard against needing anyone, the paranoid's defense is, "They're out to get me." People like Patty selectively perceive things and put unconnected occurrences together in an irrational and sometimes bizarre manner that makes perfect sense to them. If you tell Patty that her fears and paranoia are baseless or tell her she's sounding crazy, you will lose her, and you don't want that to happen. Get her to open up and tell her side of the story. Perhaps you can point out what is ridiculous about her theory in a way that hadn't occurred to her, but it might make sense enough to break through her certainty. Remember, some people have elaborate delusions that seem very real to them. You might gently mention that sometimes even when you think that people are against you, they're really not. If her delusions get in the way of her productivity and affect your work, then you may need to go to HR. This is a touchy and delicate situation. Sometimes medication is very helpful with paranoia, and when Patty comes out of her delusion, she will thank you for your help. Just get her to talk and open up to you without any confrontation.

Solution

Patty, I know you may think the boss and management have something against you. I'd really like to talk to you about it. Tell me all the signs that you see, Patty.

The Perfectionist

Situation

Petulia the Perfectionist drives everyone crazy with her micromanaging, criticism, and supervising of projects, whether she's authorized to do so or not. Many times the Petulias of the workplace are not even your boss. Similar to Mabel the Missionary and Bonnie the Bossy One who always have to be right, and to Fred who wants to convert you, Petulia just wants everyone's work to be perfect. She sees correction as a way of life and is always looking for mistakes to correct. Similar in many ways to Carson the Critic and Carl the Control Freak (both coming up), Petulia doesn't usually have the mean-spiritedness of the latter two, just the obsessive side of the first three.

Explanation

Petulia has a need to do her work correctly and is terrified of making a mistake. That alone may be frustrating for her co-workers when she's missed deadlines debating the proper use of a semicolon in her report. Petulia may suffer from OCD—obsessive-compulsive disorder, where everything has to be just so. She may also just be nitpicky, like Courteney Cox's character Monica on the TV show *Friends*. Be careful. She may have had very controlling, rigid, and perfectionistic parents and learned that in order to earn their love, she had to be perfect. Have some compassion for Petulia, and also set limits so her obsessiveness and criticism don't bug you.

Solution

Petulia, I appreciate how carefully you do your work and how you are committed to excellence. What bothers me is that sometimes your perfectionism makes you take longer than necessary and we're missing deadlines because of it. There are things that just aren't that important to debate or waste time over. Also, it seems as though you have appointed yourself the official proofreader and editor for our team. We feel that even though you do an excellent job, we also refuse to waste any more time on trivial matters when we have deadlines to meet. I hope you understand because I enjoy working with you and really appreciate your excellent work.

The Control Freak

Situation

Carl the Control Freak may be similar to Petulia the Perfectionist in his need to control, but he takes it to a more personal level. He has to have everything his way and hates to have anything interrupted, out of order, or not done the way he likes it. He may think he is everyone's boss and he's not. He can be a dictator and he must have limits set for him.

Explanation

Like Petulia the Perfectionist, Carl has to have everything just so; therefore he always tries to control the people in his world as well as every document he touches and every item on his desk. Order and organization are crucial to a control freak. Carl probably had very controlling parents and he learned how to be controlling from them. Or Carl's parents were intrusive, came into his room and disturbed the order, snooped, or took things. It was an invasion of his privacy; he resented it and swore it wasn't going to happen again so he's hypervigilant that no one disturbs his things.

Solution

Carl, I respect your dedication to dotting your i's and crossing your t's. It's reassuring to have a fellow co-worker who takes pride in his work and is committed to excellence. There's a point where I feel you slide over into the controlling sector and become overbearing. You've got to learn to be more flexible. If we change things in your report, it's not because we're disputing your data or research. If you don't agree with a change that's been made to your work, please feel free to discuss it, but it seems as though you've decided in advance to dispute any and all adjustments to your ideas, and that's just not a cooperative attitude. I'd like to get along with you and I'd like to see you succeed. I hope we can continue working together because I truly do value your input and ideas.

The Critic

Situation

Carson the Critic always looks for the flaws in your work, and in you as well. He has to point out all the errors in your reports, what you didn't address, and why your ideas are wrong, but not in a cooperative, helpful way. He likes to see the negative in everything and point it out to you, while putting you down at the same time. He generally sees his glass as half empty instead of half full. He's like Petulia the Perfectionist but with added streaks of mean-spiritedness, nastiness, and venom. But if you ever criticize Carson, he'll go through the roof because he's usually very thin-skinned. It's a one-way street with him—he gives criticism but can't take it. You have to stop him.

Explanation

Carson the Critic thinks he is perfect and has nothing wrong with him. That's far from the truth. He exemplifies the Chinese proverb, "Some people feel taller by cutting other people's heads off." You need to equal the playing field by giving him some feedback for his own good. Don't back down or let him intimidate you. Stand your ground and tell him you appreciate his feedback and it's a two-way street. He's your colleague, not your boss. His work can be open to feedback just like everyone else's. He needs to know this, so you must tell him. Limits and boundaries are important to set here with him.

Solution

Carson, I appreciate your keen eye and ear in making our output better. We depend on you for doing that. What bothers me is that your constant criticism is condescending, and it only goes one way. I'd like you to change your tone to a more conciliatory one and use phrases like, "Have you considered doing this?" or "Did you ever think of this?" When people give you *feedback, you get defensive, yell back, and shut down instead of hearing them. They may have some important contribution to make, and you're taking it so personally that you don't hear them. I'd like you to check your ego at the door and open your mind to listening to what others, including me, are saying to you. Please open yourself up to receiving feedback from others, so we can all keep submitting excellent data to the department. Thanks!*

CHAPTER 33

The Addicts

The Alcoholic/The Drug Addict/ The Addictive Personality
The Enabler/The Codependent
The Chronic Shopper
The Gambler
The Pornographer

Addiction is a disease and can involve booze, cocaine, prescription drugs, shopping, food, gambling, and sex. It also includes love, exercise, work, collecting things, hoarding, and the list goes on. Some people simply have addictive personalities. Addicts often have a genetic predisposition to addiction, so you can see it manifested across several generations. If you have an addict in your office, you should initially talk with the person individually and in private. For your conversation to be the most effective, you will need to break through his or her denial or at least plant the seed for awareness and growth. As the 12 steps say, the *willingness* to look at their addictions is the first step. Many times, addicts of all kinds have to "hit bottom" in order to recognize that their addiction is killing them.

Each addiction is a bit different, but the dynamics are the same and the approach to dealing with them is basically the same. Read up on addiction and alcoholism so you know what you're doing. When you talk to the alcoholic or addict, make sure you have materials handy: the list of rehab centers that your insurance policy covers, and the list and meeting times and locations of the local 12-step programs such as Alcoholics Anonymous (AA), Cocaine Anonymous (CA), Narcotics Anonymous (NA), Gamblers Anonymous (GA), Overeaters Anonymous (OA), Compulsive Shoppers Anonymous (CSA), Sex Addicts Anonymous (SAA), and Sex and Love Addicts Anonymous (SLAA), all of which can be found online. You may want to circle the ones that meet in the evening so you can go with the person if he or she decides to go. Be supportive yet clear and firm. Remember, addicts are in denial and need assistance, guidance, and compassion.

You may need to report their disruptive behavior to HR. Many times, HR directors and representatives are trained to address addictions—putting the person on suspension, ordering him or her into rehab, arranging with the company's insurance company to cover the treatment, working with interventionists, and other ways to support the person's recovery. Use HR's expertise to help guide you.

If the HR department won't do this, you may decide that the addict and alcoholic need an intervention, which can involve relatives, spouses, bosses, and co-workers. Get a professional interventionist to conduct such meetings. Denial is like a concrete wall, and you need to get a jackhammer to get through it. Depend on licensed professionals to help you in the process.

The Alcoholic/The Drug Addict/ The Addictive Personality

Situation

Alana the Alcoholic shows up for work drunk, hung over, sloppy, or high. Her behavior is a cry for help and she is probably in denial. Take immediate action! Her work is suffering, you find yourself covering for her, doing her work for her, and then getting blamed for her mistakes. You just can't do it anymore.

Explanation

Alana has a physiological problem and all the counseling in the world is not going to solve it until she hits bottom. She has to want to get help herself. That will only happen when she has a "moment of clarity" that her drinking is going to kill her or someone else. However, you can assist her in getting closer to that moment of clarity by confronting her, giving her support, and taking her to a 12-step program that evening.

Alcoholics and drug addicts are usually in massive denial. They minimize, rationalize, project blame on others, and tell you that they're fine. Most know the truth deep down and their outrageous behavior is actually a cry for help. They are begging people to do something because they are incapable of admitting they have a serious problem.

Solution

Alana, your work here was always excellent and in on time. Now I observe you coming to work reeking of alcohol at 9:00 in the morning, staggering in upon occasion, slurring your words, and exhibiting bloodshot eyes. Your co-workers are concerned for their safety and yours because you don't remember things. This may be a sign of blackouts, which is a sign of terminal stages of alcoholism. It's difficult for me to say this, but I think you've got a serious alcohol problem, and I'm strongly suggesting you get help and start attending AA meetings or go to rehab. If you talk to our HR representative about it, he or she will be able to accommodate you if you need to take time off while getting things together. I truly hope everything works out because I value you as a co-worker and as a person, and I'm coming from a place of respect and caring about you and for you. Will you come with me now to the HR department to discuss this?

The Enabler/The Codependent

Situation

Ernie the Enabler and Codependent usually has an alcoholic or drug addict wife or partner. He is late to work or has to leave early because of her addiction, and he tells you horror stories about her falling down, getting into car accidents, and embarrassing him when they're out in public, yet he continues to buy her booze, not checking her into rehab or bringing her to an alcohol counselor or psychotherapist. You're tired of hearing his tales of woe when he's the one aiding and abetting her awful situation.

Explanation

Ernie means well. He clearly loves his wife and wants to do what's best for her. It's hard for him to realize what exactly "the best for her" entails, though, since he has witnessed her gradual descent and is too close to the problem to view it objectively. Ernie needs to see how destructive and self-sabotaging his enabling behavior is and how his wife is getting worse and not better because of it. It might be out of line for you to suggest that Ernie get his wife some help, but that doesn't mean you can allow him to continue unburdening himself to you during work hours if you're not close, personal friends out of the office as well. If he does keep you informed of her behavior all the time, then you are within your rights to comment on it. He needs to get her help, into rehab and detox, and he needs Al-Anon groups himself. Have the list of the rehab centers and the Al-Anon meetings that you can give him when you speak with him. If he doesn't listen, you can go to HR and ask for help in somewhat the same way you did with Alana.

Solution

Ernie, I like working with you and I think you're an asset to the company. I have something important to talk with you about, though, and it is a very delicate matter. You have told me many stories about your wife's drinking and I'd hate to say it, but it sounds like she's an alcoholic. Furthermore, it seems as though you enable her by buying her booze and making excuses for her. You're not an asset to your wife and you're making her alcoholism even worse by not confronting it and by not getting her into treatment. I care about you as a co-worker, so if there's anything else I can do to help, just ask me. In the meantime, though, if you don't take my advice, I have to ask you to stop telling me stories about her behavior because it's upsetting to me. I have some literature here for you. I'd like for us to go to HR right now, because I'm genuinely worried about her health and safety and yours, too.

The Chronic Shopper

Situation

Connie the Chronic Shopper works to support her clothes habit. She's a shopaholic to the bone and it's beginning to affect you at work. She spends her lunch hour at department stores instead of eating. She interrupts you at your work to show you her purchases. Then she cries to you when she can't pay her credit card bills. You have better things to do.

Explanation

Connie has a shopping addiction. Her identity is tied up with the power she feels when she can buy something. Connie feels terrible when she doesn't look perfectly decked out in the latest designer clothes, shoes, and accessories. The movie *Confessions of a Shopaholic* had some poignant scenes of 12-step meetings with people addressing their addictive buying, which was a lighthearted way of showing that shopping actually can become a serious problem for some people. Connie shops to fill up the emptiness, loneliness, pain, trauma, childhood abuse, shame, or guilt that she feels inside like most addicts do—shopping is her drug of choice. Connie has an addiction, just like alcohol and drugs. She needs help. Get the list of the meetings of Shopaholics Anonymous and give it to Connie when you speak to her.

Solution

Connie, I like it when we work together on a project. There are times, however, when I'm working and you interrupt me to show me your latest purchases or consult on what you're planning on buying next, and it takes me away from my concentration. I don't mind weighing in every now and then, and it makes me feel good that you respect my fashion sense, but it almost seems to me like you're addicted to shopping, considering how often you've been coming by to show me outfits lately. I know you can't afford all this because you cry when you're hounded by credit card agencies. I'm concerned about that, but I have deadlines to meet also, and I need to finish my work. Please stop coming to me, and consider getting yourself some help. I have some literature here for you about Shopaholics Anonymous, and I wish you luck! I'll go with you to a few meetings if you want me to, to give you support. I know you can break through this, Connie!

The Gambler

Situation

Gavin the Gambler buys tickets for the lottery, goes to horse races, bets on sports—anything he can bet on and win money. He also is constantly on gambling websites during his lunch hour as well as on company time. He regales you with stories of how the horse he bet on almost won him $50,000 or how his lottery ticket was one number away from winning $100,000. You don't want to be bothered and it's a waste of your time hearing this. It's disturbing your work and it's got to stop. And when he asks to borrow money from you, he's in more trouble than you know.

Explanation

For Gavin, it's all about the adrenaline rush—not about winning or losing—that makes him a chronic gambler. Gavin doesn't get that he's a gambling addict and when you confront him with this fact, he will deny it and call you crazy. But if his work performance seems to be slipping, or his gambling has begun to affect you adversely at work, a confrontation is in order. Do the same thing that you did with the other addicts—get the list of meetings, times, and locations for Gamblers Anonymous (GA) and give it to him when you talk to him. He needs help, he's in denial, and you can assist him to get into recovery.

Solution

Gavin, I enjoy working with you and I'd like to keep it that way. I've noticed that you are on gambling websites during company time and that's not appropriate. I'm getting more and more concerned because I think you have a gambling addiction. You also tell me story after story about not having enough money to cover your bills. When you ask to borrow money, I know you're in trouble. I don't want to lend you money and I don't want to cover for you—I just want to see you get this problem under control. I've brought you some literature from Gamblers Anonymous. You need to go to these meetings; I'll go with you to give you some support. I'm very concerned about you. You need to take a step back from gambling and get your head back into this job. But if you're going to continue gambling, I don't want to hear another word about it. Thanks so much for listening to me. So which meeting do you want to go to tonight?

The Pornographer

Situation

Paul the Pornographer is cruising porn sites at work, even though he probably knows it's a terrible idea and is probably terrified he's going to get caught. He wastes company time being distracted by nudity online, and if you checked his cell phone, you'd probably find a lot of 900 numbers. Computer experts can track his website usage, and he should know that any company can do that within about two minutes. But how do you say something to him? Tactfully, directly, and in the same way you confronted the other addicts and alcoholics in this chapter. Have the literature ready from the Pornography Anonymous website and tell him you'll go with him to a meeting. He's in deep trouble and needs your help. You can go to HR, and tell him you will if he doesn't get help now.

Explanation

Paul has a sex addiction and is probably in denial about it. If he's doing this at the office, just imagine what he's doing behind closed doors at home. This is probably a serious cry for help—he needs someone to stop him, to get him into therapy, because he knows he needs help and he's an addict who can't stop. He may have deep-seated fear and hatred of women that comes out in his need to view pornography.

Solution

Paul, I appreciate the quality of work when we're working together. This is really embarrassing for me to bring up, but we've been co-workers long enough that I hope you trust my discretion: I've noticed that when I pass by your cubicle you're sometimes looking at porn websites. If I can see, that means everyone who passes by your cubicle can see. I don't need to tell you that this is wildly inappropriate for a workplace. If you want to look at porn, then please do it in the privacy of your home. If you don't stop it, you're going to get caught. So please stop it now. I'm sure you understand that a word to the wise is sufficient. I appreciate it. And if you don't stop it, I will go to HR. This is just not appropriate at work. I think you have a pornography addiction. Here's some literature about it, and I'm offering to go with you to a meeting tonight because I think you need it.

CHAPTER 34

The Workplace Environment

Of course, co-workers aren't the only sources of toxicity in the workplace. At offices and warehouses around the country you could notice any number of problems, including but not limited to:

- Lead paint
- Broken windows and screens
- Malfunctioning air conditioners or heaters
- Foul odors and fumes from the heating vents
- Graffiti on the walls
- Broken and leaking sinks, toilets, and water fountains
- Water on the bathroom floors
- Toilets backed up and overflowing
- Rusted and busted pipes
- Overflowing garbage and waste
- Rats, mice, cockroaches, and other pests
- Broken glass on the floors
- Burned-out lightbulbs and electricity failures
- Nonfunctioning alarm and security systems
- Dark hallways with no lighting

These conditions may be in violation of building and safety codes, may be endangering your life and that of everyone in the company, and have the potential of spreading diseases throughout the workplace. They must be remedied immediately.

Explanation

These conditions happen for various reasons:

- The company's maintenance people aren't aware of it and it's your job to bring it to their attention.
- The budget has been cut and the company's maintenance people are so overworked they didn't have time to get to it.
- Management has fired the maintenance crew and hasn't found a replacement yet.
- Management has no intention of cleaning it up, fixing it, or having a clean, safe work environment.
- The service repair people from an external maintenance company haven't arrived yet, and it may be days, weeks, or even months before it's fixed.
- The company says they have called the maintenance people but they have not.

Solution

You have many options to resolve poor working conditions. If, despite repeated requests for maintenance, there is no remedy, you can escalate your demands for repair, going down the list of actions:

1. First, immediately take photos of problem areas with your cell phone or digital camera.
2. Forward the photos to management and maintenance.
3. Contact the maintenance people and ask them to come over and fix the problem area immediately.
4. Contact the head of the maintenance company and complain directly to him or her.
5. Call and e-mail your bosses and perhaps the upper management about the matter; e-mail them the photos.
6. Contact OSHA and report it to them.
7. Photograph and videotape the poor conditions to document it. Make sure there is a time stamp on the photos and video, and post the conditions on a blog, relevant workplace safety.

violations website, YouTube, or other websites to get attention to the problem. Document this yourself immediately.

8. If management does nothing, then alert the media to the dangerous conditions and have them air a newscast segment on your poor working conditions.
9. Contact your local congressional representatives and senators—both state and national—to alert them to the conditions. You can also contact county health officials to come and look at the conditions.

Some of these actions could be seen as grounds for firing you, even if you have good intentions, are tired of waiting, and are being exposed to dangerous and toxic conditions. You may have the law on your side, though, and if you are fired, you may decide to sue your company. You may also want co-workers as witnesses, so you can have them sign a petition or have several co-workers go along with you in the plan to correct the faulty conditions. Perhaps you want them to be in the photos you take of the faulty and toxic conditions at work. Document everything and get photographs and videotape and also have other witnesses describe what they have seen.

I hope these scenarios—the situations, explanations of the psychological dynamics, and the suggested solutions—give you more insight into yourself and others, personally as well as in the workplace, so that you can take action and change the toxic circumstances at your place of work.

PART IV

STAFF INFECTIONS

What to Do After a Confrontation

CHAPTER 35

How to Heal Yourself After a Confrontation

Dealing with toxic co-workers, confronting them, and dealing with the aftermath is emotionally draining. Stress is something we all live with constantly; and it's *how* we deal with it that makes the difference. We can let it motivate us into greater achievement, growth, and wisdom, or we can get sick, buckle, and collapse under the strain. Here is some advice on how to deal with the stress in a toxic company to save your health, well-being, and sanity.

Suzanne Kobasa Ouelette, Ph.D., stress researcher at City College of New York and coauthor of *The Hardy Executive: Health Under Stress,* developed the concept of stress hardiness. She found that people who coped successfully with stress had three outstanding traits, or "The Three Cs":

- **Control.** Successful copers felt in control of their lives and decisions. They felt they could influence and have an impact on events and their surroundings and they could make things happen. They had an internal locus of control rather than an external one. They felt powerful rather than like a passive victim who allowed circumstances to dictate their life's outcome. They felt in the driver's seat of their own lives in making choices.

- **Commitment**. Successful copers also had a strong dedication, involvement, and commitment to whatever they did, put their heart into it, and gave 100 percent. They were curious about the world rather than feeling alienated from people, their workplace, or their environment.
- **Challenge.** The successful copers treated a "problem" as if it were a challenge to grow, learn, and test their strengths and abilities instead of feeling afraid, burdened, or threatened. Because they felt in control of their lives, they looked to difficult situations as something to solve and increase their skill set and expertise. As the Japanese saying goes, "The end of the world to a caterpillar is the beginning of a whole new life to a butterfly."

Combine these positive attitudes with the following healthy techniques to cope with stress and you can make your life and workplace an easier place to be. Remember, what may be stress relieving for you may be stress inducing to another! Choose methods you feel comfortable with and try new ones, too.

You must take good care of yourself in all ways all the time—mentally, physically, emotionally, psychologically, and spiritually. This is crucial to maintaining optimum health, productive work, and fulfilling relationships, especially after a confrontation. Taking care of yourself in all ways should include the following suggestions in those categories:

- **Mentally**—Meditating, visualizing, thinking positively, reading, listening to CDs and DVDs on psychological topics, expanding your knowledge and awareness, and aligning your thoughts with the highest good and most beneficial outcomes.
- **Physically**—Exercising, getting massages, taking hot showers and baths, swimming, walking, sitting in nature, deep breathing, eating lunch outdoors, going to the gym or working out with a trainer, releasing anger safely on punching bags or kickboards, joining sports teams, dancing, walking and jogging with friends or by yourself, or going to a biofeedback specialist, chiropractor,

acupuncturist, nutritionist, or other holistic health care practitioners for prevention as well as cure and relief. Taking vitamins, natural supplements, and herbs can combat stress. Drinking lots of purified water and soothing or energizing herbal teas. Getting sufficient sleep and taking naps. Stop using alcohol, cigarettes, and drugs, which destroy your brain and body and numb your ability to deal with your problems.

- **Emotionally**—Talking to supportive family and friends, playing with pets and little children, attending support groups, joining a 12-step group, such as AA, CA, NA, OA, GA, and others; beginning individual and group psychotherapy, engaging in hobbies, singing, watching movies and videos, writing in a journal, crying, and listening to soothing music, such as New Age or classical.
- **Psychologically**—Realizing your own issues and buttons that are getting pushed, understanding your co-worker's reactions, developing more objectivity about the situation, unhooking from the fear, your need for approval, and hesitation to confront them. Preparing yourself to be stronger is one of the many benefits of reading self-help books and going to counseling with a qualified mental-health professional.
- **Spiritually**—Praying, meditating, practicing yoga, and attending a church, temple, synagogue, mosque, or other place of worship; talking with your minister, priest, rabbi, shaman, imam, mullah, or spiritual advisor; taking vacations, spending alone time, and going on retreats to the beach, woods, mountains, deserts, or other places of solace and solitude of your choice to renew your soul and spirit.

When you have a conversation or confrontation with a toxic person, you may need a time to decompress, so make sure you can go to the bathroom and wash your hands and face. (Women may also want to reapply their makeup.) You may want to hide out for a few minutes by sequestering yourself in a bathroom stall. You can and should also go outside for a walk to catch your breath if you need to. Walk near a park, pond, or trees to get the negative ions generated by nature, and absorb the calming feeling of nature.

Let yourself cry if you need to, but do so away from where others can see or hear you. Some people still see tears as a sign of weakness, which they are not. Scientific research has shown that tears of sorrow contain depressants, and crying emits those from the system, so you might say, "Oh, I feel so much better after a good cry." And you do! The body has automatic ways of restoring itself to a positive state, and tears are one way it does that, so let yourself cry if you need to. Holding in the tears only deepens the depression, sadness, and frustration, and can lead to emotionally caused ailments such as headaches, migraines, back and neck problems, constipation, nausea, and other somatic complaints.

Directly following a confrontation or conversation, write down exactly what you remember happened—what you said, what the other person said, the order in which it was said, and the emotional tone. Immediate memory is more reliable than long-term memory. This may be important when you send your follow-up e-mail or letter, outlining the details of your conversation, with the resolutions of things that you both may have promised to change. If this confrontation results in a report to HR, disciplinary action, mediation, or a lawsuit, you need to have the facts written down and in order very quickly because you will need as much documentation as possible.

You may want to send your follow-up letter or e-mail to the person soon after the encounter. This will show your commitment to resolving the problem and will give you the chance to thank the person for speaking with you. Outline what was said and the changes that you both agreed to. If you want to and if you both agreed to do this, send it to your immediate superiors if that is appropriate. In case of a future lawsuit, this may be submitted as evidence, so be very careful about your wording.

Your account of what happened should be as chronological as possible, with each of your points numbered for easy reference, in case this is ever used by HR, attorneys, judges, or in court. For example, after the standard greeting and the "thank you for meeting with me," outline the way the encounter and the discussion progressed; for example:

The following is an account of my perceptions of what transpired after I asked you to meet with me on Tuesday, April 21, 2009, at 3:00 P.M. to discuss your habit of not having your work done on time and how it affects me and everyone in our department.

1. You have not had your work done on time, and this has been occurring for the past three weeks, and it is no longer tolerable.
2. I told you the specifics of your missing work from the proposal for the Haines Project and how it is affecting the Development department.
3. I asked you if you needed an assistant or help from me or anyone in the department.
4. You stated you could get it done by yourself and did not need any help.
5. I then asked you to have it done the following day, Wednesday, April 22, 2009, by 10:00 A.M.
6. You agreed and said it would be done and handed in to me the next day on Wednesday, April 22, 2009, by 10:00 A.M.
7. You did not complete the work and did not turn it in to me by 10 A.M. the next day on Wednesday, April 22, 2009.
8. Despite my repeated requests and your constant litany of personal problems and car repairs, your work still isn't turned in.
9. Your part of this proposal for the Haines Project is essential and only you have the data for your section.
10. As I stated, you leave me no choice but to report this to our boss and to HR.

Sincerely,

Alice Norris
Project Supervisor

Using this format spells out any future action that needs to be taken and ensures that you have outlined the progression of events and are covered. The next step is up to HR.

As a co-worker or project manager, you are responsible to move things along to successful completion, and Mike has been preventing you from doing so. You offered him assistance from an aide and from others in the department as well as your own help, which he declined. You have done your part. Let HR take over from here. You may be called in to a meeting by yourself or with Mike to resolve this. Be open, honest, forthcoming, and understanding.

When you return home, take a walk in the park or around the neighborhood, get to the gym and work out, go for a ride on your bicycle, take a hot bath or a hot shower, make a cup of relaxing tea, play some restful music. Take care of yourself and go to bed early. A good night's sleep is restorative to the body's cells after something that may have been frightening or fraught with difficulty or anxiety. Wake up and get ready for the next day at work!

Be prepared for any repercussions, rumors, avoidance from co-workers, gossips, or people pumping you for confidential information. Be pleasant, tactful, and firm, stating that you can't discuss the matter and that you hope all will be resolved soon.

CHAPTER 36

How to Heal Co-Workers After a Confrontation

Once you have taken care of yourself, helping to heal co-workers after a confrontation is crucial, especially if your co-workers overheard the conversation or were in the same room. Word travels fast, and many times the entire company will have heard about it within minutes—and definitely within twenty-four hours. You will need to cover yourself, do some damage control, and put psychological salve on any wounds. If the encounter was a heated exchange with raised voices that was witnessed by co-workers, speak to each one individually and reassure him or her that you are all right and that you are working out your difficulties with your co-worker. Your colleagues need to know that you are OK and that you are a strong, positive, and resolute person who is committed to having a pleasant, cooperative working environment for yourself and for others. You may even want to bring in some cookies or muffins for your co-workers, or you may want to send them an e-mail with a general comment about what happened. (Be careful—it may be used in a lawsuit.)

If it was a heated argument and many co-workers heard it, then be direct and don't try to sweep it under the carpet, since it's possible someone will have a photo or video of two people screaming at each other. Write something like, "Rachel and I had a lively exchange about our issues, and I feel we will continue to discuss our differences of opinion until we reach a resolution. I thank you for your e-mails, phone calls, voice messages, text messages, and in-person support over the past day." Bringing in treats is a way to show your gratitude, to display that you're fine, and to show that you are exhibiting a positive attitude about resolving your differences.

You may want to share the stress management techniques spelled out in Chapter 35 with your co-workers so they can rest, heal, and decide what they would like to do and how they would like to handle the situation.

CHAPTER 37

What to Do If You Need Help from HR or Management

If you have gone to your supervisor or the HR person to ask him or her to mediate, a wise boss and a good HR representative will call each party into his or her office separately and privately to hear both sides of the story and then set an appointment for both parties to be in the same discussion session in which they will mediate the communication. Many times, bosses like to handle this by themselves, and some even pride themselves on being good mediators. Other bosses really don't want to get in the middle of two co-workers; they will gladly and quickly notify the HR director to take over, and the HR director will then handle this alone. Sometimes the corporate attorney will be present to add gravitas to the discussion if it's serious and to head off future lawsuits. Many HR representatives do not like to nor encourage the corporate attorney to be present and they discourage you from bringing an attorney to any informal grievance. They want to avoid any semblance of a possible lawsuit.

If you feel more comfortable bringing legal representation with you, you may want to do that. You may meet resistance from the HR director; your HR representatives may also not inform you whether the corporate attorney will be present, even if you ask. They may surprise you and have the attorney there anyway. Or they may decide at the last minute to bring in the corporate attorney to cover themselves. Some may be ordered to do so by the company president or their own boss. Each company has its own policy and procedures about grievance matters. For informal meetings, it may just be an individual meeting with each person, and then a meeting with both parties to see if it can be resolved without any lawyers coming in to the meeting.

After the HR representative gathers facts and investigates the complaint, he or she usually will issue a letter stating the ruling. This may include spelling out the resolution. It may also state if there is a suspension, firing, or further discussions between the aggrieved parties to avoid a lawsuit. The representative may want to personally conduct these discussions. He or she may also refer the situation to the EAP counselors to handle and report on. Or HR may sweep it under the carpet, stall for time, and go through the motions just to look good.

If the complaints are egregious and the corporate attorney has been informed of such—as in sexual harassment cases, racial or gender discrimination, and so on—then the attorney may recommend a settlement to avoid a lawsuit. If you don't like what HR has ordered, you may be able to appeal to higher-ups. You may also decide to sue. Be careful you don't sign any documents where you promise *not* to sue. Do not accept a settlement or cash a check that prohibits you from taking it to a higher level or to the courts. Endorsing and cashing the check may mitigate and negate your right to sue if you sign an agreement that contains such provisions. Be careful and always bring any document before your attorney to read and decode what it says since the language can be very confusing to an ordinary person without the legal expertise.

CHAPTER 38

What to Do If Administration and HR Don't Do Their Job

If your administration and HR refuse to do their job by handling and resolving the difficulty, you have various alternatives. Here is a brief list with the details and specifics of each choice:

- Go to higher-ups—boss, boss's boss, department head, district manager, regional manager, president, CEO, COO, board of directors, and other executives.
- Go to your Employee Assistance Program (EAP).
- Get into counseling or therapy.
- Go to the Equal Employment Opportunity Commission (EEOC).
- Go to the Occupational Safety and Health Administration (OSHA).
- Go to trade associations and professional organizations.
- Go to your union.
- Seek legal advice.
- Threaten legal action.
- Take legal action.
- Go to the media.
- Become a precedent-setting law case.

If you can think of other actions, please contact me and I will add them in any future editions of this book. Thank you!

Go to Higher-Ups

If HR and your immediate supervisor have not been able to resolve your issues satisfactorily, you may be forced to go to their bosses. Depending on the structure of the company, that may be another supervisor, or if it is a small company, you may go to the vice president or even the president. Follow all the previous suggestions: ask for private, confidential, uninterrupted time; bring in your notes and any evidence such as e-mails and letters; and tell the person what you would like to have resolved and in what ways. He or she hopefully will then call in the other party and have a private conversation with that person without you there. Then the higher-up will schedule an appointment for both of you to come in at the same time to resolve the issues. If you do this, it may be the perfect solution. On the other hand, if the person favors your co-worker, doesn't understand your plight, or tries to cover it up, you may not get the issues resolved and be forced to go even higher up the administrative chain, or you may need to get an attorney.

Go to Your Employee Assistance Program (EAP)

If you go to your EAP to discuss your work situation, please know that the EAP usually works for and is hired by the company, so your records may not be totally confidential. They may even side with the company against you. In a court of law, your EAP therapist and counselor can be subpoenaed to testify, and your records may be submitted as evidence. Sometimes EAP counselors may not like to do court work and you must be honest with them from your first appointment that it is a possibility that your case could go to court. Find one who is comfortable with going to court.

Get into Counseling or Therapy

Going to a private, licensed counselor or psychotherapist rather than an EAP enables you to maintain your confidentiality. You may want to keep the fact that you are going to counseling totally private so it is inadmissible in court. However, if the opposing attorney finds out, he or she may want to subpoena the records. So make sure that the counselor or psychotherapist is aware that he or she may be called on to appear in a court of law about your case if it goes that far and that you have his or her agreement to testify. Many counselors and psychotherapists do not like to go to court and will not take you on as a client if that is the case. They may refer you to another counselor or therapist. Other counselors and psychotherapists relish court work and are very prepared to take detailed notes of your sessions in case they must make an appearance. If you have an insurance policy paid for by the company, you may only have to be responsible for a co-pay, which can be as little as ten or twenty dollars. However, you may prefer to not put anything through your insurance company and pay the full amount in cash rather than a check in order to not have a bank record of checks for your private counseling sessions, because in a lawsuit all of your bank records may be submitted as evidence. Whether or not your insurance company pays for your counseling sessions, the opposing side may subpoena the therapist's records for a law case. If your insurance is through your company, it can be a double bind.

Go to the Equal Employment Opportunity Commission (EEOC)

If your disagreement is a matter for the EEOC, this may be a better, more efficient, and more powerful way to handle the situation for you than a lawsuit. Most attorneys take a percentage of the case—anywhere from 20 to 60 percent—in addition to court costs, filing fees, etc. Filing with EEOC will save you on legal fees, retainers, and court costs because the EEOC is a government agency. The drawback is that many EEOC offices have been closed or had services cut because of government budget restraints; but if you can find an office and a commissioner who will handle your claim, it may be the best solution for your problem. Most companies do not want to have the stigma of being reported to the EEOC to besmirch their name.

You have an advantage if your case qualifies to be taken on by the EEOC. If you work for a federal, state, county, or local government agency or for a business, company, or corporation that takes federal funding or has to answer to a government agency, such as a TV and radio station reporting to the FCC; or if it is a social-services agency and has to answer to the state and county as well as to federal guidelines; and if it trades, does business with, or is funded by the government, such as a public school, community college, or state university, then its license may be suspended or not be renewed, its funding may be cut, or its agency may be closed because of frequent reports of discriminatory behavior.

These are some government agencies that can help you in filing any complaints:

Equal Employment Opportunity Commission (EEOC)—eeoc.gov
Americans with Disabilities Act (ADA)—ada.gov; 1-800-514-0301
U.S. Department of Justice—usdoj.gov; fax: 1-202-307-1198

Go to the Occupational Safety and Health Administration (OSHA)

If there are dangerous workplace situations or noncompliance with building or safety codes, such as faulty wiring or plumbing, asbestos, broken glass, broken structures; outdated and decrepit equipment, safety apparel, shoes, boots, helmets, etc.; OSHA is the government agency to report it to. Here is the contact information for any complaints: osha.gov; 1-800-321-OSHA.

Go to Trade Associations and Professional Organizations

Legal counsel, which you may get for free if you don't have money for the lawsuit, can be available through your union, professional or trade association, political party, the ACLU, the NAACP, Southern Poverty Law Center, N.O.W. and the Women's Defense League of the National Organization for Women, or attorneys and law firms who take pro bono cases because they have a commitment to fairness, justice, and their altruistic leanings. Find "friends of the court" who will bolster your case by writing briefs on your behalf. You may even find enough other complainants to make it a class-action suit, from people who have been wronged by a company's misdeeds, pollution, lies, sexual harassment, or racial, gender, ethnic, or sexual preference discrimination.

Go to Your Union

Unions usually have a legal department that handles complaints such as discrimination, unfair treatment, and so forth. If you belong to a union, you will not be charged attorney fees. The union attorney will send letters and file any complaints with the court to bring your case to resolution. This may be the best solution for you if your budget is tight and if you need to put more pressure on the company to settle your dispute. Most companies do not want the negative publicity or to be thought of as unfair to their employees, which can restrict their hiring, productivity, and approval of government licenses and/or government contracts.

Seek Legal Advice

You may need to seek legal advice from a qualified, licensed attorney who has a specialty in employment or business law. Many do not charge for an initial consultation, while others lower their fee for the first appointment. If you have to hire a private attorney, many will ask for a retainer up front, which could be several thousand dollars. Other attorneys will take the case on a contingency basis, and they will take a percentage of the final monetary judgment that you win. That means if they take a third, and you win $100,000, they will get $33,333, and you will get $66,667. Make sure when choosing an attorney that he or she has the experience, contacts, education, dedication, and specialty licensing that will help you win your case.

Threaten Legal Action

You can write a letter to your supervisor, or even go to the next higher level of executives or to the top level of executives, and describe what the problem is. You may hire an attorney to write a letter that threatens the company with legal action. Sending a letter from an attorney on his or her stationery can provide the power and authority that you need to get your company to negotiate with you. Most companies do not want the public exposure and costs of a trial. A letter from your attorney may put pressure on your company to settle the case with you out of court.

I'd like to share a case with you. An older woman was finishing her doctoral dissertation at a prestigious university. Her dissertation committee was composed of all men. They continued to reject her writing, postpone her oral examination, and generally make her life miserable for years. It was way too long for her to be dealing with their passive-aggressiveness and their blatant sexism against her. I recommended that she hire a local attorney to send them a letter to threaten them with a sexual discrimination lawsuit and to use any statistics that could prove that men who had doctoral dissertations were not delayed for years in their quest to have their orals scheduled. For the cost of perhaps two or three hours of an attorney's time—which included review of her records and correspondence, preliminary phone calls, letter writing, and follow-up—she might be able to avoid a costly lawsuit against the university. She took my advice and found an attorney who wrote the university a letter with a cc to each of the committee members. Within a week or so, her oral exam was scheduled, she passed with flying colors, and she was awarded her Ph.D. Assertiveness was the key.

Take Legal Action

If going to your supervisor, writing a letter, and even having an attorney write a letter all fail, then have the attorney file a law case with the courts and go to the media to generate publicity to get the situation corrected. What companies do not want is bad publicity, so they will negotiate with you to settle the case. If the company does not respond, or if they have written to your attorney that they refuse to settle, you may need to proceed with legal action. Please know that this will probably be a long and involved process and that their attorneys will go to great lengths to discredit you, humiliate you, bring out any secrets, and engage in character assassination. The opposing attorney may hire private investigators to follow you, document your comings and goings, dig into your past and present, and place overwhelming pressure on you. You need to be strong, to have a solid emotional support system to cope with the pressure, and to believe in your cause to withstand the negativity. Corporations and companies may deliberately stall and drag the case on for years to wear down your resolve, hoping you or your attorney will fail to meet certain filing dates or run out of money, stamina, and willpower. If you prevail, it will be well worth the battle to right the wrong. Many companies have been forced to pay millions of dollars in sexual harassment and sex discrimination lawsuits, as well as racial and gender discrimination cases. Some cases have gone all the way to the Supreme Court and have even set precedents. You can be a trailblazer if your case is significant enough.

During settlement negotiations, the opposing side may include a clause in the settlement agreement that is similar to a "gag order." They may try to prevent you from writing a book about the incident, turning it into a TV movie or film, going to the media, or appearing on any TV or radio shows or doing interviews with magazines, e-zines, or bloggers. Make sure your attorney tells you your rights and that you know exactly what you are agreeing to and signing, because in some cases, if you violate the terms of the agreement, you may have to return any settlement money to the company. If you plan on writing a book about your case, turning it into a TV movie or film, or making any media appearances and granting interviews, then make sure your settlement agreement allows you to do so.

Remember that attorneys usually take 40–60 percent of your final settlement as their fee, plus you have to pay the fees of the expert witnesses, process servers, court reporters, photocopying and mailing/courier costs, travel expenses, and so forth. To understand what you may experience, view the movies that have been made from real-life lawsuits, some of which have made legal history, righted wrongs, and set precedents. See Precedent-Setting Law Cases later in this chapter for a list of feature and made-for-TV films. If you have others to add, please contact me at Linnda.Durre@gmail.com.

When several people file a lawsuit, there is power in numbers. These are called *class-action lawsuits*, and many times these cases set legal precedent and can benefit all of the people in the company and throughout the country. Expert legal help, especially for class-action suits, can be found through national and state bar associations, researching cases on the Internet, and finding the original attorneys and law firms of the plaintiffs. Many times local magazines have features such as "Best Attorneys in Town"; check them out with the state bar, search for them on the Internet, and ask former clients for reviews. Call and interview them on the phone, and find out their track record. Many times they take these cases on a contingency fee, so not much money is coming out of your pocket for these cases. Some attorneys have a free or low-cost thirty- to sixty-minute consultation to listen to you about your case, read your documents, and then decide whether to take you on as a client.

Resolutions

Resolving a minor conflict with a co-worker can make your office a much better place to work and give you the self-confidence and peace you were seeking. Depending on what action you take, you may win a monetary reward, set a precedent in case law, be reinstated (if fired), perhaps with back pay; right a wrong for yourself and others in your company and across the country, or have enough money to live comfortably, start your own business, or retire. Whatever you do, be prepared to cope with stress, difficult times, frustrations, delays, character assassination, deceit, backstabbing, losing friends and colleagues, and self-doubt, all of which may be worth it if you emerge victorious.

Go to the Media

You need to be careful if you decide to take this step, because the media can be a double-edged sword. There are many wonderful, ethical, crusading TV and radio reporters and investigative journalists who are committed to helping right the wrongs of society, to helping the underdog, and to exposing crimes. Just look at what Bob Woodward and Carl Bernstein did to expose President Richard Nixon's lies and corruption in their reporting on Watergate. There are also unscrupulous, unethical journalists who will exaggerate, sensationalize, and take things out of context to sell newspapers, tabloids, and magazines and to boost TV and radio ratings. Proceed with caution. Media exposure can also garner you witnesses who see and read about the story and come forward to back up your case with additional testimony. These people may even become fellow plaintiffs in a class-action suit. Perhaps they didn't have the proof, resources, attorney, or individual bravery to go it alone but now feel bolstered by your filing, so there is strength in numbers.

Become a Precedent-Setting Law Case

If you have a difficult co-worker or boss who is not getting the message and changing his or her toxic behavior, you don't have to hire Vinnie and Guido to rough him or her up or outfit the difficult person with a pair of concrete shoes to swim with the fishes. What you need to do is bond with others in your company who may have experienced the same toxic behavior you have, despite repeated requests for change. Remember, some complaints have turned into precedent-setting Supreme Court cases, like *Brown v. Board of Education*, which eliminated the "separate but equal" fallacy in our schools, or *Harris v. Forklift Systems*, which changed the landscape for sexual harassment cases forever. You can research many other cases on the Internet involving discrimination, harassment, and other workplace violations.

These cases changed the lives of millions of people in the United States and even prompted legislative and legal changes in other nations across the globe. Your last name could be in the title of the case that rocked the judicial world to help millions of people who have been wronged. Your name will be in the law books forever as the brave person who rose to the challenge to change an unfair law or a system that discriminated against a certain group. The following sections will tell you how to do that.

Who knows? They might even make a feature film or a TV movie out of your story. Here's a brief list of some of the most powerful true-life stories, most of which were made into films or TV movies:

- In November 1996, after dragging on for two and a half years, Texaco Inc. signed what may have been the largest settlement of a racial discrimination lawsuit, agreeing to pay an immediate $115 million in damages plus pay raises of at least 10 percent to about 1,400 black employees. An unusual aspect of the settlement, valued by plaintiffs' lawyers at $176 million in all, called for Texaco to form a seven-member "equality and tolerance task force" that will give the plaintiffs a say in hiring and promotion policy at the giant oil company. The case was settled in ten days of urgent negotiations that began November 12, 1996, the day after the disclosure of secret recordings of senior Texaco executives denigrating black workers and plotting to destroy incriminating evidence in the lawsuit.

- *Erin Brockovitch*, starring Julia Roberts, who won an Academy Award for Best Actress in the title role, Aaron Eckhart, and Albert Finney. Brockovitch, a young woman and mother, investigates the pollution by a major company of a water source for an entire community where the residents report higher cancer rates, birth defects, and miscarriages than the general population. She won the case and was hired by the law firm, Masry and Vititoe, as a researcher. Erin Brockovich now serves as director of research at Masry and Vititoe, where she is currently involved in other major environmental lawsuits (speaking.com/speakers/erinbrockovich.php).
- *All the President's Men*, starring Dustin Hoffman, Robert Redford, and Jason Robards Jr. Two young investigative reporters, Bob Woodward and Carl Bernstein, track down and expose the lies and corruption of President Richard Nixon and his associates to reveal the Watergate scandal, guided by their *Washington Post* editor, Ben Bradlee.
- *Silkwood*, with Meryl Streep in the title role of Oklahoma nuclear plant worker Karen Silkwood, who discovered and blew the whistle on dangerous practices at the Kerr-McGee plant where she worked. Silkwood died under mysterious circumstances that are still being debated. Also starring Cher, Craig T. Nelson, and Kurt Russell.
- *Marie*, starring Sissy Spacek in the title role as Marie Ragghianti, a former Tennessee Parole Board chair, who had been fired from her job. Ragghianti claimed it was because she refused to release

felons after they had bribed aides to Democratic Governor Ray Blanton in order to obtain clemency. Actor and former U.S. Senator Fred Thompson, who was her attorney at the time, played himself in the movie. In 1977, he filed a wrongful termination suit on her behalf against Blanton's office. During the trial, Thompson and Ragghianti discovered and exposed the cash-for-clemency scheme that led to the ousting of Blanton from office. In July 1978, a jury awarded Ragghianti $38,000 in back pay and ordered her reinstatement.

- *North Country*, starring Charlize Theron, a semifictionalized account of the women miners at the Eveleth Mines in Minnesota who sued the mining company for sexual harassment and discrimination because of the hostile work environment. Their case, *Jenson v. Eveleth Mines*, was finally won after a long, protracted legal battle, and it became the first sexual-harassment lawsuit in history to be given class-action status. Oscar winner Theron was nominated for a Best Actress Academy Award for this film, which is based on Lois Jenson's true story and the book *Class Action: The Story of Lois Jenson and the Landmark Case That Changed Sexual Harassment Law*, by Clara Bingham and Laura Leedy Gansler.
- *A Civil Action*, starring Robert Duvall, Kathleen Quinlan, William H. Macy, and John Travolta as attorney Jan Schlichtmann, who filed the case of *People of Massachusetts v. W.R. Grace*. W.R. Grace was a company that owned a leather-processing factory that had been dumping a cancer-causing industrial solvent into the water table of Woburn, Massachusetts, for more than a decade, resulting in the deaths of several children.
- *Gideon's Trumpet*, a TV movie starring Henry Fonda, about Clarence Gideon, an indigent man who was not given his full legal rights and his fight to be appointed counsel at the expense of the state. This landmark case led to the Supreme Court's decision that extended this right to all criminal defendants.
- *With All Deliberate Speed*, a documentary by Peter Gilbert that unearths the legacy of the landmark Supreme Court decision in *Brown v. Board of Education*. In this case it was ruled that "in the

field of public education, the doctrine of 'separate but equal' has no place." The movie includes never-before-heard stories from people directly responsible for, and greatly affected by, the original case.

- *The Rosa Parks Story*, starring Angela Bassett as Rosa Parks, whose refusal to move to the back of the bus led to the Montgomery bus boycott and ignited the modern civil rights movement; and *Boycott*, starring Jeffrey Wright as Rev. Martin Luther King Jr., which also is about the Montgomery bus boycott.
- *Serving in Silence: The Margarethe Cammermeyer Story*, starring Glenn Close as Colonel Margarethe Cammermeyer, a closeted lesbian who had served in the military for more than twenty years. In 1989, during a routine interview to upgrade her security clearance rating, she told the investigator that she was a lesbian. The "don't ask, don't tell" policy was not yet in effect at the time. The National Guard began proceedings to discharge her, and she was honorably discharged on June 11, 1992. She decided to fight for her right to serve and filed a lawsuit against the decision in civil court. In June 1994, Judge Thomas Zilly of the federal district court in Seattle ruled that her discharge, and the ban on gays and lesbians serving in the military, was unconstitutional. She returned to the National Guard and served as one of the few officially accepted openly gay or lesbian people in the military until her retirement in 1997.
- *Roe v. Wade*, starring Amy Madigan as attorney Sarah Weddington, who headed the legal team in defending the legal rights of plaintiff Jane Roe, played by Holly Hunter, in the case that made abortion legal based on the right to privacy.
- *Milk*, starring Sean Penn in an Oscar-winning performance as the title character, Harvey Milk, who became the first openly gay city councilman for San Francisco. As city supervisor, Milk was the driving force behind the passage of a gay-rights law that prohibited discrimination, or unequal treatment, in housing and employment based on sexual orientation. At his urging, the city announced a drive to hire more gay and lesbian police officers. He also started programs that benefited minorities, workers, and

the elderly. Milk then gained national attention for his role in defeating a state senate proposal that would have prohibited gays and lesbians from teaching in public schools in California.

- *Brubaker*, starring Robert Redford as Henry Brubaker, new warden of Wakefield prison, who disguised himself as an inmate before taking over the prison so he could see and experience firsthand the corruption and scams the guards and prison officials were running. When he revealed himself and started to implement reforms to stop the corruption, the local community businesses, which had been benefiting from the scams, fought back and joined forces with the corrupt southern prison system to make political trouble for the new warden. He fought for laws regarding prison reform.
- *And the Band Played On*, an HBO movie and true story about the first reporting, tracing, and discovery of HIV/AIDS, starring Alan Alda, Matthew Modine, Richard Masur, and others, based on the book by investigative journalist Randy Shilts. This has led to the enactment of laws regarding the reporting of HIV/AIDS.
- *On the Waterfront*, starring Marlon Brandon, Eva Marie Saint, Rod Steiger, and Lee J. Cobb. This film exposed the illegal activities of corrupt officials of the dockworkers' union and led to federal and state inquiries.
- *The Laramie Project*, an HBO docudrama about the murder of Matthew Shepard, a young gay man in the Wyoming town of Laramie, starring Stockard Channing and Sam Waterston as his parents, Judy and Dennis Shepard. The incident led to the passage of the Matthew Shepard Local Law Enforcement Hate Crimes Prevention Act.

CHAPTER 39

Summary and Conclusion

Confronting these dysfunctional, obnoxious, and difficult types at work can be challenging, especially if you're shy, conflict averse, or have never been able to stand up for yourself. Things happen for a reason, and certain people are placed in your path to teach you a lesson, inspire you, and challenge you. They are there to help you face your own problems, to confront your own areas of necessary growth, and to propel you to greater accomplishments. Perhaps that is why the woman next to you who is constantly talking on the phone about her personal life is there. After putting up with behavior that drives you crazy, you reach a breaking point; you need to stand up for yourself! And your taking action can help the other person, who may need limits, goals, and discipline to correct her rude, disturbing, unethical, or even illegal behavior.

Some companies and corporations have wonderful, cooperative, and responsive bosses and HR departments. They listen to employee complaints and do their best to remedy toxic situations and environments as quickly as possible. I congratulate them and hold them up as examples to business and industry everywhere.

This book is for those working at companies and corporations that are lazy, corrupt, and negligent and that ignore dangerous situations and toxic people who harm their employees. What they don't understand is that they are losing money, damaging morale and their reputation, and making things worse. Your bosses, the HR department, the higher-level executives, and the company can attempt to silence you and others, by sweeping problems under the carpet, circling the wagons, discrediting you, attempting to minimize the damage, and any other egregious transgressions to squelch your complaints. So instead of handling it quickly and effectively within the company in a win/win manner, their avoidance or negligence prompts your legal action, which may result in negative publicity, the potential loss of millions of dollars in profits, plummeting stock value, and a severely damaged reputation from which they may never recover. If mediation is recommended, perhaps you can work out the differences without a costly lawsuit.

I hope that you have supportive colleagues, bosses, HR departments, and companies that will have the integrity and ethics to deal with the challenges in the workplace that need to be addressed and corrected for the betterment of their employees, the environment, the planet, and the future of their companies. Let me paraphrase a sentence attributed to visionary inventor, designer, and architect Buckminster Fuller: "The future of the planet depends on each person's individual integrity."

Besides being a business and corporate consultant, I've been a licensed psychotherapist for thirty-one years as well as a national speaker and trainer, adjunct college professor, intern supervisor, author, writer, journalist, newspaper and magazine columnist, and TV and radio talk-show host. During that time, I've dealt with many problems and challenges, which I've written about, hosted and produced TV and radio shows on, and discussed in speeches, seminars, workshops, and lectures. Taking questions from the audience is one of my favorite things to do. At one of my appearances, a businessman in the back of the room stood up and said, "You're the only psychotherapist I've ever heard who doesn't answer a question with another question! Thank you for that!"

My response to him and to you is that if I were a client—either in counseling, psychotherapy, or in business consultation—I would want direct and helpful answers, feedback, suggestions, options, and resources. Information is power, and my job is to give people, corporations, and businesses more information so they can evaluate the situation; look inside themselves and their companies; explore their strengths, feelings, weaknesses, deficits, and fears; and then come to a decision about their action plan and implement it for positive and productive change. I hope this book does that.

Follow these examples and look at the supplemental materials on my website and in the Bibliography—read the books, listen to the audiotapes and CDs, watch the DVDs—and they will enrich your assertiveness skills, give you more communication techniques, and increase your bravery to confront and stop toxic situations in your workplace all by yourself. Take my workshops and attend my speeches and seminars. My corporate and business consultation services are also available. Please contact me at 407-739-8620 or Linnda.Durre@gmail.com; my website is www.DrDurre.com.

I welcome e-mails, suggestions for the next edition, descriptions of toxic types that I overlooked in this book, and any legal cases that I should add that were instrumental in changing laws to protect workers from dangerous workplaces, obnoxious people, and threatening situations. I wish you courage, strength, and assertiveness in your discussions, mediations, and confrontations.

Acknowledgments

To my late parents, Catherine and Theodore, and my sister, Lois—thanks for the rocket fuel! To her son, my nephew Joshua—I loved playing with you when you were a baby!

At McGraw-Hill: my book publisher, Judith McCarthy; senior editor, John Aherne; project editor, Joseph Berkowitz; production supervisor, Craig Bolt; production artist, Pamela Juárez; publicist, Julia Baxter; marketer, Kenya Henderson; cover designer, Tom Lau; copyeditor, Katherine Hinkebein; and everyone there who contributed to making this book the best it could be.

To my literary agent, Jacqueline Varoli Grace, founder of LifeTime Media, Inc.; editors past and present who worked on my book: Dorothy Spencer, Karyn Gerhard, Kevin Moran; and the staff and interns—Natalie Way, Stephanie Baeza, Angela Vidalis, and others. Deborah Day; William P. Strachan; my managers, Bernie and Suzanne Lax; and book publicists, Pam Lontos and Rick Dudnick, and their staff at PR/PR: Patricia Kleir, Amanda Tucker, Russell Trahan, and Martha Ciske.

My office manager and bookkeeper, Frances M. Clay; Mardy and Katherine Grothe; Jane Starets and her late husband, Richard; Kenneth B. Wheeler; Christel Wight; Edward Soulsby; Sheila El-Musrati; Kristin Lippens; Pippi Howard; Linda Caponegro; Tim Colley; Ruth Griffin; Carol Halliburton; Marci Elliott; Sandra Milliner; Beverly Safier; Annie Kidwell; Rita Sahakian Das; Karen Trudeau; Eric Reiss; Robert Perry; Christina Dorrer; Steve Matchett; Barry Sandler; Geralyn Motto; Janet and Joe McWilliams; Doug Basham; Lydia Cornell; Dick Batchelor; Todd and Joanne Persons; Carol and Bill Schaefer; Anna Bresnahan; Fraser Bresnahan; Regan Wesnahan; Leib Lehmann; Rolf Gompertz; Leonard Goodstein and Jeanette Goodstein; Marian York; Betty Frain; John and Margie Faessel; Mick and Phyllis Meagher; Alan Swartzberg; Barbara Spargo; Susie Pecuch; Ed Asner and his assistant, Patty Egan.

Jim and Pam Ray, Joan Endsley, Jim Gregory, Kathleen Isaac, Vincent Cilurzo, John Purdy, Rich Brownstein, Ken Boyle, Jerry Schiefelbein, Joanie King, Marge and John Wood, Britt Smith, Bruce Lindsey, Carl Grumer, and Elliott Grumer. Helene and Reno Zinzarella and all my teachers from kindergarten through graduate school; Robert Hess and Raymond F. Bacchetti, of Stanford University; Kerry Stratford, Michael Cardona; American Reprographics, Marilyn Bell, Photo Scan, Greg Young, Fred Zara, John Weyrick, Patricia and Brad Fuller, John Dussling, Jason Brown, Lisa Garthwaite, Erik Reiss, Noel Osment, Peggy Collins, Barbara

Fischer, and all my assistants at my former La Jolla office; Michael Milder, Maureen McGee Milder, Russell Fahrenkamp, Audrey Hope, Dale Reynolds, Amy and Bill McDermott, Sheila Richardson, David Wilkening, Marie Cusick, Jamie Cusick, Ann Vitelli, Marge and George Gough, Dorothy and Peter Carone, Jody and Ron Gorneau, Charles "Pat" and Carol Pagliuca; Barbara and Dan Dubek; her children, Christopher, Lauren, and Danielle; her son-in-law, Jim Lynch; and her daughter-in-law Heather Wittig Dubek.

My beloved late mentor, Marilou Conner; her son, Tim Conner; and his father, Jim Conner; Mary Lou Sunderwirth Conner, Elizabeth Prince, Sheree Bennett, Paul Bard Michaels, Reba Runyan, Alan Matez, Sue Devito, Jimmy White, Nanncy House and Lee, Robert Heyges, Bart and Debbie Shepherd, Rob Sharpstein, Jan Leach, Victor Soto, Alba Vales, Carl Foreman, Charles Rahn, Christina Lopez Morgan and Jerry Morgan, Jacqueline Roberge, Phel Steinmetz, Alicia Rodriguez; Jim Hicks; Drs. Lillian Harvey Banchik and Mark Banchik, Linda Crowley, Lorenzo Hill, Mike Vestal, Desiree Lewis, George Hopkins, Roxanne Furman, Beatrice Montoya and her family, Joseph Maddox, Brad Lemack, Julia Ledbetter, Jennifer Jefcoat, Barbara Rowe, Roger Perron, Terri Hixon, Evelyn Coughlin, Jennifer Bennett, Geri Dahl, Karen Morrice, Mary Jane and Yime Otani, Judy and Dave Christensen, Carl Kumpf, Helen Kerrigan, Henry Vales, Kimbrough Jennings, Gene Romangna, Kim Courtney, Rachel Hamman, Raven McElman; everyone at WEUS: Carl Como, Carl DiMaria, Tom Brook, Doc Burkhart, Kristen L. Howard, Ron Tosches, Doug Basch, Raul Pantoja, Jose Miranda, Heidi Ayala, George Crossley, Doug Guetzloe, and Bobbie DePew; Roger Moore at the *Orlando Sentinel*; Kathi Belich and everyone at WFTV; plus Bill Baumann, Ed Rose, Amanda Ober, Todd Husty, and everyone at WESH; Cynthia Landers and everyone at WOFL; everyone at WKMG; Jackie Brockington and everyone at Central Florida News 13; and everyone in the media in Orlando; Kenneth Cogburn, Cindy Barth, Bill Orben, Susan Lundine, Steve Doyle, and everyone at the *Orlando Business Journal*; Jennifer Crespo, Caroline Ross, Julie Fioretti, Gary Hughes, Jim Phillips, Curtis Gee, Sandy Knickerbocker, Christopher Esposito, Anastasia Colondres, Dustin Infinger, Kristen Heimburg, Jesse Baguchinsky, Adam Maldonado; everyone in the Orange County and Osceola County Public Schools and Javier Melendez, Carol Johnson; Larry Rowan, Pamela Strickland, Jim Bird, Nate Fancher, Paulette Swanson, and Mr. Estes; Matthew Abalos; Merrie Cunningham, Nancy Gaylean, and Eleanor Cain.

My interns, both past and present: Adam Arnali, Alexandra Buxo, Alyssa Garofalo, Amid Williams, Amy Meier, Arianna Stewart, Ashley Dean, Babita Persaud, Caitlyn McKinzie, Cara Jacob, Carlyne Jean-Baptiste, Casarah Henderson, Christina Greco, Cristina Montes, Dana Mooney, Diana Rigatuso, Dominic Digennaro Markewitz, Eydia Portillo, Falecia Duncan, Frances Lambert, Jaede Brereton; Janique White, Jayne Green, Jennifer Harman, Jennifer Reed, Jennifer Snow, Jessica Britos, Jessica Gonzales, Julie Popolow; Kalem Jones, Kate Cavinder, Kenneth De La Flor, Krystle McMullan, Leanne Taylor, Lindsay Weinstock, Lois Hemm, Maha Chaudhry, Marlaine Monroig, Michelle Benavides, Monica Slocum, Nicole Avery,

Nicole Tiffany Smith, Paula Ibanez, Sarah Roberts, Shane Westmoreland, Shelda Raymonvil, Sinitta Lindsay, Stephanie Rios, Tatiana Isis, Tomas Negron, and Zara Malik.

Mick and Phyllis Meagher, Mary and Alan Swartzberg, Barbara Spargo, Suzen and Michael Scures; Dale Reynolds, Eric Waldron; Brandy Foster, Tina Munroe, Angela Robison, Brent DelaCruz, Fung Soong, Philippe St. Leger, Emre Selimata, Stella Kalachi, John Kalachi; Sandy Knickerbocker, Chris Esposito, Adam Maldonado, Jesse Baguchinsky, Dustin Infinger, Kirstin Heimburg, Anastasia Colondres; Ken Williams; Kevin Williams; David Jackson; Frances Jackson; Maggie Rogers, Tom Nance, Christina Dorrer, Robert Perry, Bob Lavallee, Jonathan Chambers, Jonathan Giles Zimmerman, Megan McInnis; Denise Moore, Karen Mottarella, Stacey Dunn, Terri Hernandez, Bryan Zugelder, Karen Cox; Barry Sandler, Dale Reynolds, Sharon Fleming, John and Margie Fleming, Rita Manyette, Cindy Hogan, Diane Ladd, and Aine McIteer.

Ed Donovan and Ann Waisanen; Steve Elmes, Bill Matthies; Sarah and Bob Solmor and family; Keith Kirkwood, David Cameron, and Tomas Link; Marsha McCollough, Nick Clayton, and Ada Mojita.

The late Gregge Tiffen; his wife, Bonnie Beck Tiffen; the late George Dillinger; Barbra and Michael Makay, Rama Berch, Anita Sands, Donna DeVerniero, Patti Love, Laurie Schryver, Jill Cook, Carol Adams, and the late Donna Salk.

Mario Marsilio, Tony Marsilio, Sherry Wingler; Mary Cole, Paul Jacoy, Gene Orlovsky, David Campanelli, Dietrich Dragton; Joseph E. Fuller and his assistants, Debby Hanson and Jennifer; Byron Moore; Lynn Lombardo; Alberto deArriagoitia, Gerald Renato, Joe Vomero, Cliff Wagner, Lance Farber, Nicolai Lennox, Michael Greenberg, Peter Eartheart, Doug Hankins, Richard Bame.

Kathleen McSilvers, J Jackson, Veronica Sommers; Marvin and Joan Terry; Erika Mueller; Ann Boroch and her assistant Tina; Mary Lou Rane; and Eve Campanelli; Edgar Acune; Gigi Samuels, Sharon McKinney, Suzi Hewitt, Diane Valentin, Candy Stewart, Tammi Ferreira; and James Outlaw; Maxine Tabas; Suzette Gore, John Hou and his assistants Nelly Santos and Cynthia Arvelos.

Lawrence Haber, Alan D. Davis, Mark Cooper, Hillary Bibicoff, Richard Citron, David Deutsch; Carl Grumer, Hal Cooper; Karla Shippey and staff; Frank Keasler, Joseph Seagle, Arvind Mahendru, Lou Comeau, Ron Sims, Todd Stern, Nicole Weaver, Brett Smith, Gregg Smith, Lance Rosen, Heidi Isenhart, Heather Kirson, Kathryn Ross and staff.

I thank my readers who have bought my books, CDs, DVDs, audiobooks, merchandise, and materials. I hope it brings you understanding, peace, and love. Think positive, communicate, be tenacious, work it out, and know that everything has its place in God's timing. If I have accidentally left out a name, please forgive me. I thank all of you in the acknowledgments and those I have not mentioned because each one of you has contributed to my knowledge, learning, growth, and enlightenment.

Bibliography

A comprehensive bibliography of my book topics is found on my website: www.DrDurre.com.

Alcoholism and Drug Addiction

Beem, Charles, and Joseph A. Califano Jr. (The Healing Project). *Voices of Alcoholism: The Healing Companion: Stories for Courage, Comfort and Strength*. Brooklyn, New York: LaChance Publishing LLC, 2008.

Meagher, David. *Beginning of a Miracle: How to Intervene with the Addicted or Alcoholic Person*. New York: HCI, 1987.

Washton, Arnold M. *Willpower's Not Enough: Recovering from Addictions of Every Kind*. New York: Harper, 1990.

Wholey, Dennis. *The Courage to Change*. New York: Time Warner, 1984.

Anger Management

Evans, Patricia. *The Verbally Abusive Relationship: How to Recognize It and How to Respond*. Avon, Mass.: Adams Media, 1996.

Harbin, Thomas. *Beyond Anger: A Guide for Men*. New York: Avalon, 2000.

Hightower, Newton, and David Kay. *Anger Busting 101*. Houston: Bayou Publishing, 2002.

Nay, Robert. *Taking Charge of Anger: How to Resolve Conflict, Sustain Relationships, and Express Yourself Without Losing Control*. New York: Guilford, 2004.

Body Language

Andersen, Peter. *The Complete Idiot's Guide to Body Language*. Indianapolis: Alpha Books, 2004.

Goman, Carol Kinsey. *The Nonverbal Advantage: Secrets and Science of Body Language at Work*. San Francisco: Berrett-Koehler, 2008.

Hagen, Shelly. *The Everything Body Language Book: Master the Art of Nonverbal Communication to Succeed in Work, Love, and Life*. Cincinnati: Adams Media, 2008.

Hargrave, Jan. *Strictly Business: Body Language: Using Nonverbal Communication for Power and Success*. Dubuque: Kendall/Hunt, 2001.

Hartley, Gregory, and Maryann Karinch. *I Can Read You like a Book: How to Spot the Messages and Emotions People Are Really Sending with Their Body Language*. Franklin Lakes, N.J.: Career Press, 2007.

Hartley, Mary. *Body Language at Work*. London: Sheldon Press, 2003.

Hogan, Kevin. *The Secret Language of Business: How to Read Anyone in 3 Seconds or Less*. Hoboken, N.J.: John Wiley & Sons, 2008.

Johnson, Annette R. *Employee Body Language Revealed: How to Predict Behavior in the Workplace by Reading and Understanding Body Language.* Ocala, Fla.: Atlantic, 2009.

Karlins, Marvin, and Joe Navarro. *What Every Body Is Saying: An Ex-FBI Agent's Guide to Speed-Reading People.* New York: HarperCollins, 2008.

Kuhnke, Elizabeth. *Body Language for Dummies.* West Sussex, U.K.: John Wiley & Sons, 2007.

Lambert, David. *Body Language 101: The Ultimate Guide to Knowing When People Are Lying, How They Are Feeling, What They Are Thinking, and More.* New York: Skyhorse Publishing, 2008.

Pease, Allan, and Barbara Pease. *The Definitive Book of Body Language.* New York: Random House, 2004.

Reiman, Tonya. *The Power of Body Language: How to Succeed in Every Business and Social Encounter.* New York: Pocket Books, 2007.

Tieger, Barbara Barron, and Paul D. Tieger. *The Art of Speed Reading People: How to Size People Up and Speak Their Language.* New York: Little, Brown, 1998.

Internet Addiction

Careaga, Andrew. *Hooked on the Net.* Grand Rapids, Mich.: Kregel Publications. 2002.

Greenfield, David N. *Addiction: Help for Netheads, Cyberfreaks, and Those Who Love Them.* Oakland: New Harbinger Publications, 1999.

Young, Kimberly. *Caught in the Net: How to Recognize the Signs of Internet Addiction—and a Winning Strategy for Recovery.* New York: John Wiley & Sons, 1998.

Narcissism

Behary, Wendy T. *Disarming the Narcissist: Surviving & Thriving With the Self-Absorbed.* Oakland: New Harbinger, 2008.

Bernstein, Albert. *Emotional Vampires: Dealing with People Who Drain You Dry.* New York: McGraw-Hill, 2001.

Martinez-Lewi, Linda. *Freeing Yourself from the Narcissist in Your Life.* New York: Jeremy P. Tarchner/Penguin, 2008.

Payson, Eleanor. *The Wizard of Oz and Other Narcissists: Coping with the One-Way Relationship in Work, Love, and Family.* Royal Oak, Mich.: Julian Day, 2002.

Sex, Love, Pornography Addiction, and Employee Theft

Beattie, Melody. *Beyond Codependency: And Getting Better All the Time.* Center City, Minn.: Hazelden, 1989.

———. *Codependent No More: How to Stop Controlling Others and Start Caring for Yourself* (2nd ed.). Center City, Minn.: Hazelden, 1992.

Carnes, Patrick, David L. Delmonico, Elizabeth Griffin, eds. *In The Shadows of the Net: Breaking Free from Compulsive Online Sexual Behavior.* Center City, Minn.: Hazelden, 2007.

Carnes, Patrick J. *Out Of the Shadows: Understanding Sexual Addiction.* Center City, Minn.: Hazelden, 2001.

Shulman, Terrence. *Biting the Hand That Feeds: The Employee Theft Epidemic.* Haverford, Pa.: Infinity Publishing, 2005.

Psychopathic, Sociopathic, and Antisocial Personalities

Babiak, Paul, and Robert D. Hare. *Snakes in Suits: When Psychopaths Go to Work.* New York: HarperCollins, 2006.

Black, Donald W., and C. Lindon Larson. *Bad Boys, Bad Men: Confronting Antisocial Personality Disorder.* New York: Oxford University Press, 1999.

Clarke, John. *The Pocket Psycho.* Milsons Point, N.S.W.: Random House Australia Pty. Ltd., 2008.

———. *Working with Monsters.* Milsons Point, N.S.W.: Random House Australia Pty. Ltd., 2005.

Hare, Robert D. *Without Conscience: The Disturbing World of the Psychopaths Among Us.* New York: Guilford, 1993.

Kantor, Martin. *The Psychopathy of Everyday Life: How Antisocial Personality Disorder Affects All of Us.* Westport, Conn.: Praeger, 2006.

Visualization, Manifesting, and Creating the Life You Want

Bristol, Claude M. *The Magic of Believing.* New York: Pocket Books, 1948.

Bry, Adelaide. *Visualization: Directing the Movies of Your Mind.* New York: Macmillan, 2006.

Cooper, Philip. *Secrets of Creative Visualization.* York Beach, Maine: Red Wheel/Weiser, LLC, 1999.

Dyer, Wayne W. *You'll See It When You Believe It: The Way to Your Personal Transformation.* New York: HarperCollins, 1989.

Friedman, Martha. *Overcoming the Fear of Success.* New York: Warner, 1988.

Hay, Louise. *You Can Heal Your Life.* Carlsbad, Calif.: Hay House, 1984.

Hill, Napoleon. *Master Key to Riches.* Northbrook, N.Y.: Ballantine, 1965.

———. *Think and Grow Rich.* Northbrook, N.Y.: Random House, 1960.

Jeffers, Susan. *Feel the Fear and Do It Anyway.* New York: Ballantine, 2006.

Patent, Arnold M. *You Can Have It All.* New York: Pocket Books, 1995.

Peale, Norman V. *The Power of Positive Thinking.* New York: Prentice-Hall, 1952.

Sher, Barbara, and Annie Gottlieb. *Wishcraft: How to Get What You Really Want.* New York: Ballantine, 1986.

Shinn, Florence S. *The Game of Life and How to Play It.* London: Random House UK, 2004.

Sinetar, Marsha. *Do What You Love, The Money Will Follow: Discovering Your Right Livelihood.* New York: Dell, 1989.

Index